101 Things To Do With an Instant Pot®

101 Things® To Do With an Instant Pot®

BY DONNA KELLY

GIBBS SMITH
TO ENRICH AND INSPIRE HUMANKIND

First Edition

23 22 21   10 9 8 7

Published by
Gibbs Smith
P.O. Box 667
Layton, Utah 84041

1.800.835.4993 orders
www.gibbs-smith.com

Designed by Virginia Snow
Printed and bound in Korea

Gibbs Smith books are printed on either recycled, 100% post-consumer
waste, FSC-certified papers or on paper produced from sustainable PEFC-
certified forest/controlled wood source. Learn more at www.pefc.org.

Library of Congress Cataloging-in-Publication Data

Names: Kelly, Donna, 1955- author.
Title: 101 things to do with an instant pot / Donna Kelly.
Other titles: One hundred one things to do with an instant pot
Description: First edition. | Layton, Utah : Gibbs Smith, 2019. |
Includes   index.
Identifiers: LCCN 2018037062 | ISBN 9781423651178 (spiral-bound pbk.)
Subjects: LCSH: Pressure cooking. | LCGFT: Cookbooks.
Classification: LCC TX840.P7 K45 2019 | DDC 641.5/87--dc23
LC record available at https://lccn.loc.gov/2018037062

With love and admiration to Amy Kelly Welsh,
for her excellence and creativity in testing
the recipes for this book. And—oh yes—for
her patience as my daughter and friend!

www.gibbs-smith.com

CONTENTS

Poultry

Apricot Pineapple Chicken Thighs 64 • Whole Roasted Chicken with Vegetables 65 • Huli Huli Chicken 66 • Honey Garlic Chicken 67 • Chicken Cordon Bleu Pasta 68 • Herb Butter Turkey Breast 69 • Chicken Broccoli Casserole 70 • Sticky Asian Chicken Thighs 71 • Chicken Curry in a Hurry 72 • PB&J Chicken Thighs 73 • Chicken Burrito Bowls 74 • Indian Butter Chicken 75 • Kung Pao Chicken 76

Fish and Seafood

Vera Cruz Fish Fillets 78 • Asian Caramel Salmon 79 • Mediterranean Fish Stew 80 • Pecan Crusted Halibut 81 • Tuna Noodle Casserole 82 • Shortcut Seafood Paella 83 • Southern Shrimp and Grits 84

Vegetarian Entrees

Weeknight Mac and Cheese 88 • Vegan Southwest Quinoa Bowls 89 • Cheese Ravioli Lasagna 90 • Coconut Curry Lentils 91 • Vegan Mushroom Masala 92 • Pizza Topped Frittata 93 • Lentil Sloppy Joes 94 • Shortcut Stuffed Peppers 95 • Coconut Curry Cashew Rice 96 • Stacked Cheese Enchiladas 97 • Warm Beet Salad 98

Side Dishes

Low Maintenance Risotto 100 • Boston Style Beans 101 • Fluffy Mashed Root Vegetables 102 • Lemon-Pistachio Spaghetti Squash 103 • Braised Red Cabbage 104 • Quick Polenta 105 • Salt Crusted Fingerling Potatoes 106 • Cinnamon Orange Sweet Potatoes 107 • Speedy Spanish Rice 108 • Twice Cooked Potatoes 109 • Cauliflower Au Gratin 110

Sweet Treats

Five Ingredient Flan 112 • Fudgy Chocolate Cake 113 • Coconut-Cinnamon Rice Pudding 114 • Vegan Lemon Poppy Seed Cake 115 • Classic Key Lime Pie 116 • Chocolate Cheesecake 117 • Rave Reviews Cheesecake 118 • Upside Down Berry Cobbler 119 • Walnut Banana Cake 120 • Miracle Strawberry Jam 121 • Effortless Dulce de Leche 121 • Pineapple Upside Down Cakes 122 • Cinnamon Roll Bread Pudding 123 • Cinnamon Red Hots® Applesauce 124 • Everybody's Favorite Caramel Corn 125

HELPFUL HINTS

The Instant Pot® will revolutionize the way you cook!

Gone are the days when cooking with old school stovetop pressure cookers was a risky thing. Once upon a time, you could wind up with a delightful dinner on the table or with your dinner exploded onto the walls and ceiling of your kitchen. The Instant Pot® is an electric pressure cooker—and so much more—that is safe and easy to use.

This cookbook focuses on easy, family friendly recipes with simple cooking instructions, a minimum of prep time and few ingredients, usually ten or less. All the recipes in this book were tested and cooked in the Instant Pot® Duo Plus 6 Quart.

1. The Instant Pot is a busy home cook's best friend! It is a "set and forget" appliance that will make getting food on the table painless and almost effortless. You can cook beans and whole grains without having to soak them for hours, cook frozen food in no time, and cut prep and cooking time to a fraction of what they normally are.

2. Budget friendly cooks love the savings that come from buying inexpensive cuts of meat that cook down to melt-in-your-mouth tender in very short cooking times.

3. The wonderful thing about the Instant Pot® is that so many features are combined into one appliance. For example, you can sear your food first and then leave it in the Instant Pot® and finish your dish using the pressure cooking feature. This creates less mess, and most importantly, keeps all the flavor in one sealed container—making your food so much more flavorful.

4. The Instant Pot® pressure cooking feature works best with at least one cup of liquid as part of the recipe. Or, if you have a recipe using vegetables that release water during cooking, you will need less liquid.

5. You will get good results and shorter overall cooking times if the ingredients are hot when you turn on the pressure cooking feature. For this reason, many of these recipes call for starting with the Sauté function and heating the ingredients as the first step.

6. Additional equipment that is used in this cookbook:
   • 6- to 8-cup capacity, ovenproof glass bowl
   • An 8-inch springform pan fits perfectly into the Instant Pot® if it has no "lip" at the bottom. A 7-inch springform pan works well with all the recipes in this book.
   • 8-inch round wire trivet with handles
   • 8 ounce ramekins

7. One way to release pressure from the Instant Pot® is to let the pressure release slowly. If you choose this option, then at the end of the pressure cooking time, the Instant Pot® will automatically switch to Keep Warm, and the timer will start showing how much time has passed from when the pressure cooking stopped. Some recipes call for a period of time when using natural release, or just specify an amount of time to let it sit. With this method, the food will continue to cook during the Slow Pressure Release time.

8. Another method to release pressure from the Instant Pot® is Quick Pressure Release. This means to turn the pressure valve located on the top of the lid to "release" or "venting," at which point steam will be released from the Instant Pot® very quickly. When all the pressure is released, the silver button on the top of the Instant Pot® will drop and make a clicking sound. The lid will then open and the food inside will stop cooking sooner than with the Slow Pressure Release method.

APPETIZERS

CROWD PLEASER
SPINACH ARTICHOKE DIP

1 jar (6 ounces)	**artichoke hearts**
4 cups	**loosely packed chopped spinach leaves**
1 1/2 cups	**water,** divided
1/2 cup	**sour cream**
8 ounces	**cream cheese,** at room temperature
1 cup	**grated Monterey Jack cheese**
1 tablespoon	**cayenne pepper sauce**
1 teaspoon	**salt**
1 teaspoon	**garlic powder**
1/2 teaspoon	**pepper**
	tortilla chips, crackers, crostini, or cucumber slices, for serving

Drain the liquid from the jar of artichokes into a mixing bowl. Dice the artichokes and add to the bowl. Add the spinach, 1/2 cup water, sour cream, cheeses, pepper sauce, salt, garlic powder, and pepper; stir together until well-combined.

Spray a 6–8-cup ovenproof glass bowl with nonstick cooking spray. Spoon mixture into the bowl and cover loosely with aluminum foil. Pour remaining 1 cup of water into the Instant Pot®. Place bowl on a wire trivet and lower the trivet into the pot. Place lid on pot and lock into place to seal. Cook on Normal Pressure for 12 minutes. Use Quick Pressure Release. Serve with tortilla chips, crackers, crostini, or cucumber slices, as desired. Makes 8–10 servings.

TANGY ASIAN
LETTUCE WRAPS

¼ cup	**honey**
¼ cup	**hoisin sauce**
¼ cup	**rice vinegar**
2 tablespoons	**Sriracha or other hot sauce**
2 tablespoons	**soy sauce**
3 cloves	**garlic,** minced
2 tablespoons	**grated fresh gingerroot**
2 pounds	**boneless pork shoulder,** cut into 3-inch chunks
2	**green onions,** thinly sliced
¼ cup	**chopped roasted peanuts**
I head	**Bibb lettuce**

In a small bowl, whisk together the honey, hoisin sauce, vinegar, hot sauce, soy sauce, garlic, and ginger; pour into Instant Pot®. Add pork chunks and stir to coat.

Place lid on pot and lock into place to seal. Cook on High Pressure for 20 minutes. Use Quick Pressure Release. Press Cancel and turn to Normal Sauté. Remove pork to a cutting board and let cool. Whisk and cook contents in pot until liquid is reduced by half, about 5 minutes.

When pork is cooled down, shred with 2 forks and add to reduced sauce; toss to coat. Serve topped with onions and peanuts, wrapped in individual lettuce leaves. Makes 6–8 servings.

HASSLE-FREE HUMMUS

1 cup	**dried chickpeas**
4 cups	**water**
1 pinch	**baking soda**
4 tablespoons	**olive oil,** plus extra for garnish
4 tablespoons	**tahini***
1/3 cup	**lemon juice**
3 cloves	**garlic,** minced
1 teaspoon	**salt**

Add chickpeas, water, and baking soda to Instant Pot®. Place lid on pot and lock into place to seal. Cook on High Pressure for 40 minutes. Use Quick Pressure Release.

Drain the chickpeas, reserving the cooking liquid; set aside to cool. Place chickpeas, 4 tablespoons oil, tahini, lemon juice, garlic, and salt in a blender; blend until smooth. While blender is on, slowly stream in the reserved cooking liquid until hummus reaches desired consistency, using about ¾ cup. Spoon into a serving bowl and drizzle oil over top, if desired. Makes 4 cups.

*Found in the condiments or ethnic food section of larger grocery stores.

BUFFALO CHICKEN DIP

2 packages (8 ounces each)	**cream cheese,** softened
$\frac{1}{2}$ cup	**blue cheese salad dressing**
$\frac{1}{2}$ cup	**sour cream**
$\frac{1}{2}$ cup	**water**
2 cups	**finely shredded cooked chicken**
$\frac{1}{2}$ cup	**Buffalo sauce, or cayenne pepper sauce**
2 cups	**grated Monterey Jack cheese**
2	**green onions,** whites and greens, cut in $\frac{1}{4}$-inch-thick slices
	tortilla chips or crackers, of choice

Place all of the ingredients except chips in a large bowl and mix well to combine. Spoon into Instant Pot®. Place lid on pot and lock into place to seal. Cook on Normal Pressure for 10 minutes. Use Quick Pressure Release. Serve with chips or crackers. Makes about 5 cups.

INSTANT DEVILED EGGS

1 cup	**water**
6	**large eggs**
2 tablespoons	**mayonnaise**
1 tablespoon	**extra virgin olive oil**
2 teaspoons	**mustard**
	salt and pepper, to taste
	garnishes, of choice

Pour water into Instant Pot®. Place wire trivet in pot and arrange the eggs on top of trivet. Place lid on pot and lock into place to seal. Press the Egg setting, or cook on High Pressure for 8 minutes. Use Quick Pressure Release. Peel eggs while running under cold water and place in a bowl of very cold water to chill.

Cut eggs in half lengthwise, remove yolks, and place in a small bowl. Add the mayonnaise, oil, and mustard and mash together until very smooth. Season with salt and pepper. Fill egg whites with yolk mixture and top with desired garnishes. Chill until ready to serve. Makes 12 deviled eggs.

Variations:
Spicy Asian Style. Replace the oil with Sriracha sauce and top with sesame seeds.
California Style. Replace mayonnaise with mashed ripened avocado. Top with crumbled bacon.
South of the Border Style. Replace mustard with hot sauce, of choice. Top with a thin slice of jalapeno pepper.

CRANBERRY CHICKEN WINGS

1 can (14 ounces)	**jellied cranberry sauce**
2 tablespoons	**frozen orange juice concentrate**
1/3 cup	**cayenne pepper sauce**
1 tablespoon	**soy sauce**
2 1/2–3 pounds	**chicken wings** (about 24 pieces), wing tips removed
1 tablespoon	**cornstarch mixed with 2 tablespoons water**
	salt and pepper, to taste

In a large bowl, whisk together the cranberry sauce, juice, pepper sauce, and soy sauce. Add wings and stir until completely coated. Pour wings and any remaining sauce into Instant Pot®. Place lid on pot and lock into place to seal. Cook on High Pressure for 10 minutes. Use Quick Pressure Release. Press Cancel.

Preheat oven broiler.

Arrange wings on a large baking sheet in a single layer. Broil until lightly browned in patches, keeping a close eye on wings so as not to burn. Turn wings and broil other side.

Skim fat from top of liquid in pot and turn to Normal Sauté. Bring to a boil and cook, stirring occasionally, until mixture is reduced by half, 5–8 minutes. Whisk in cornstarch mixture. Return to a boil, stirring constantly until glaze has thickened, 1–2 minutes. Season with salt and pepper. Toss wings with a little of the glaze and serve with remaining glaze on the side. Makes 24 wings.

BREAKFAST

VEGGIES AND EGGS IN RAMEKINS

I tablespoon	**butter**
I ½ cups	**diced vegetables,** such as onion, celery, or peppers
I teaspoon	**salt,** divided
½ teaspoon	**pepper,** divided
I cup	**water**
6	**large eggs**
6 tablespoons	**cream**
⅔ cup	**grated cheddar cheese**

Turn Instant Pot® to High Sauté and let heat for about I minute. Add butter, vegetables, ½ teaspoon salt, and ¼ teaspoon pepper. Stir and cook until vegetables are softened and lightly browned, about 3 minutes. Press Cancel. Remove vegetables and rinse out inner pot. Add water and place a wire trivet into the pot.

Spray 6 (6 ounce) ramekins with nonstick cooking spray. Divide the cooked veggies between the ramekins. Crack I egg into each ramekin and sprinkle with remaining salt and pepper. Top each egg with I tablespoon of cream and a little cheese. Place 3 ramekins onto the trivet. Arrange the 3 remaining ramekins on top of the first 3, alternating the placement so that they straddle the ramekins on the bottom.

Place lid on pot and lock into place to seal. Cook at Low Pressure for I–3 minutes, depending on how runny you like your egg yolks. Use Quick Pressure Release. Remove ramekins from pot and serve immediately. Makes 6 servings.

TATER TOT®
BREAKFAST CASSEROLE

6 ounces	**cooked breakfast sausage links,** cut into ½-inch-thick slices
I tablespoon	**vegetable oil**
2 cups	**grated cheddar cheese**
4 cups	**frozen Tater Tots®**
½	**red bell pepper,** diced
3	**green onions,** thinly sliced
6	**large eggs**
½ cup	**milk**
I cup	**water**

Turn Instant Pot® to Normal Sauté. Add oil to the pot and let heat for 1–2 minutes. Add the sausage and cook, stirring occasionally for 3–5 minutes, until browned. Press Cancel. Remove sausage to a large bowl. Wipe out pot with a paper towel.

Add the cheese, tots, bell pepper, and onion to the sausage and toss together. Spray an 8-inch springform pan with nonstick cooking spray and spread sausage mixture evenly in the bottom. In a medium bowl, whisk together the eggs and milk and pour evenly over mixture in pan; do not stir. Cover pan loosely with aluminum foil.

Pour water into pot. Place pan on wire trivet and lower into pot. Place lid on pot and lock into place to seal. Cook on High Pressure for 10 minutes. Use Quick Pressure Release. Makes 4–6 servings.

HUEVOS RANCHEROS

2 tablespoons	**vegetable oil,** divided
4 (6 inch)	**corn tortillas**
1 cup	**enchilada sauce**
2 tablespoons	**tomato paste**
$\frac{1}{2}$ cup	**cooked pinto or black beans**
1 cup	**grated cheddar cheese,** divided
4	**large eggs**
	garnishes, of choice, such as salsa, sliced green onions, or diced jalapeno peppers

Turn Instant Pot® to Normal Sauté. Add 1 tablespoon oil and heat for about 1 minute. Place 1 tortilla in the pot and cook for about 1 minute on each side, or until slightly crispy. Repeat with remaining tortillas, adding a little oil each time. Press Cancel and wipe out pot with a paper towel.

In a small bowl, whisk together the enchilada sauce and tomato paste. Pour 1/2 cup of sauce evenly into bottom of an 8 inch springform pan. Arrange tortillas on top of sauce, overlapping to fill bottom of pan. Pour 1/2 cup of sauce over tortillas, spreading evenly to cover. Sprinkle beans and 1/2 cup cheese over top. Crack eggs over cheese and sprinkle remaining cheese over eggs, drizzling any remaining sauce on top. Cover loosely with aluminum foil, place on a wire trivet, and lower into the pot. Place lid on pot and lock into place to seal. Cook on Normal Pressure for 5 minutes. Use Quick Pressure Release. Serve garnished as desired. Makes 4 servings.

MASON JAR OMELETS

2 cups	**diced cooked vegetables,** of choice
I cup	**diced cooked meat,** of choice, optional
I cup	**grated cheese,** of choice
8	**large eggs**
½ cup	**milk**
½ teaspoon	**salt**
I cup	**water**

Spray 4 wide-mouth pint-size Mason jars with nonstick cooking spray. Add to each jar ½ cup vegetables, ¼ cup meat, if using, and ¼ cup cheese.

In a medium bowl, whisk together the eggs, milk, and salt. Pour ½ cup of egg mixture into each jar, using a fork to gently mix contents together. Cover each jar loosely with aluminum foil.

Pour water into Instant Pot®. Arrange all 4 jars on a wire trivet and lower into the pot. Place lid on pot and lock into place to seal. Cook on Steam setting, or at Low Pressure for I0 minutes. Use Quick Pressure Release. Carefully remove hot jars from pot. Makes 4 servings.

Variations: Denver Omelet. Use diced bell peppers, onions, chopped fresh tomatoes, ham, and cheddar cheese.
Mushroom Omelet. Use diced cooked mushrooms and onions, and Swiss cheese; omit the meat.
Southwest Omelet. Use diced bell or mild chile peppers and onions, chorizo, and pepper Jack cheese.

APPLE CINNAMON STEEL CUT OATS

I can (14 ounces)	**coconut milk**
I cup	**applesauce**
I cup	**steel cut oats**
1/2	**large sweet apple,** unpeeled, grated or finely diced
1/3 cup	**maple syrup**
I teaspoon	**cinnamon**
I teaspoon	**vanilla**
1/4 teaspoon	**salt**
1/2 cup	**chopped walnuts**

Spray Instant Pot® with nonstick cooking spray. In a medium bowl, mix all the ingredients together except walnuts and pour into the pot. Sprinkle walnuts on top.

Place lid on pot and lock into place to seal. Cook on High Pressure for 30 minutes. Let sit for 10 minutes. Use Quick Pressure Release. Makes 6 servings.

PINEAPPLE UPSIDE DOWN OATMEAL

1 can (20 ounces)	**pineapple tidbits**
1 jar (10 ounces)	**maraschino cherries**
⅓ cup	**brown sugar**
1½ cups	**old fashioned rolled oats**
1 can (14 ounces)	**coconut milk**
1 pinch	**salt**

Drain the can of pineapple, reserving the juice. Drain and chop the cherries. Scatter the pineapple, cherries, and sugar in the bottom of the Instant Pot®.

In a medium bowl, stir together the reserved juice, oats, milk, and salt. Pour into the pot. Place lid on pot and lock into place to seal. Cook on Normal Pressure for 8 minutes. Use Quick Pressure Release. Run a knife around the edge of the oatmeal to loosen and carefully invert onto a serving platter. Makes 6–8 servings.

EGGS BENEDICT CASSEROLE

6	**English muffins,** split and cut into 1-inch pieces
3	**green onions,** cut into 1/2-inch-thick slices
8 ounces	**Canadian bacon slices,** chopped
6	**large eggs**
2 cups	**milk**
1/2 teaspoon	**cayenne pepper sauce**
1 teaspoon	**salt**

Quick Hollandaise Sauce

1 cup	**plain Greek yogurt**
2	**large eggs**
2	**egg yolks**
1 teaspoon	**salt**

Preheat oven broiler.

Arrange muffin pieces on a baking sheet and toast under broiler until golden brown, watching carefully so as not to burn. Place in a large mixing bowl with onions and bacon; toss. In a medium bowl, whisk together the eggs, milk, and pepper sauce. Pour egg mixture over bread and stir to coat. Let sit for 10 minutes, stirring occasionally until most of the liquid is absorbed.

Spray Instant Pot® with nonstick cooking spray. Pour bread mixture into pot. Place lid on pot and lock into place to seal. Cook on Normal Pressure for 20 minutes. Let sit for 10 minutes. Use Quick Pressure Release. Serve with hollandaise sauce. Makes 4–6 servings.

For the Quick Hollandaise Sauce, turn clean Instant Pot® to Normal Sauté. Add yogurt, eggs, and egg yolks. Whisk until completely blended. Cook to desired thickness; add salt. If the mixture is too tart stir in a pinch or two of sugar.

FRENCH TOAST CUPS

4	**large eggs**
2 cups	**milk**
1 teaspoon	**vanilla**
8 cups	**stale French bread cubes**
1 cup	**water**
	syrup or fruit topping, of choice

Spray 6 (8 ounce) ramekins with nonstick cooking spray.

In a large bowl, whisk together the eggs, milk, and vanilla. Add the bread and toss to completely coat. Let sit for 1–2 minutes and toss again, making sure that all the liquid has been absorbed. Divide the soaked bread cubes evenly between each of the ramekins, filling them to the top.

Pour water into the Instant Pot®. Place 3 of the ramekins on a wire trivet and lower into the pot. Arrange the remaining 3 ramekins on top of the bottom ones, alternating so they straddle the edges. Place lid on pot and lock into place to seal. Cook on High Pressure for 8 minutes. Let sit for 10 minutes. Use Quick Pressure Release.

Preheat oven broiler.

Place ramekins on a baking sheet, and broil for 1–2 minutes to lightly brown tops watching closely so as not to burn. Serve with syrup or fruit topping, as desired. Makes 6 servings.

FAMILY SIZE BUTTERMILK PANCAKE

1 ½ cups	**flour**
1 teaspoon	**baking powder**
¼ teaspoon	**salt**
1 cup	**buttermilk**
2 tablespoons	**butter,** melted
1 cup	**water**
2	**large eggs**
3 tablespoons	**sugar**
2 tablespoons	**vegetable shortening or butter**
	favorite pancake toppings

In a mixing bowl, whisk together flour, baking powder, and salt. In a separate bowl, whisk together the buttermilk, butter, water, eggs, and sugar. Stir wet mixture into the dry ingredients until well-combined.

Spread shortening or butter in the bottom and 2 inches up the sides of the Instant Pot® and pour in the batter. Place lid on pot and lock into place to seal. Cook on Low Pressure for 40 minutes. (If your Instant Pot® has a Cake setting, use that instead of Low Pressure.) Let sit for 10 minutes. Use Quick Pressure Release.

To remove pancake, run a rubber spatula around the edge of the pancake and quickly invert onto a serving plate. Cut into wedges and serve with toppings, of choice. Makes 4–6 servings.

Variation: For a super quick version of this recipe, use 3 cups of prepared batter from an instant pancake mix. Melt 2 tablespoons butter and stir into batter; proceed with the recipe, starting with the second paragraph.

BLUEBERRY RICOTTA BREAKFAST CAKE

5	**large eggs**
¹⁄₂ cup	**sugar**
2 tablespoons	**butter,** melted
³⁄₄ cup	**ricotta cheese**
¹⁄₂ cup	**plain yogurt**
I	**lemon,** zested
I teaspoon	**vanilla**
³⁄₄ cup	**flour**
¹⁄₄ cup	**cornmeal**
¹⁄₂ teaspoon	**salt**
2 teaspoons	**baking powder**
I cup	**fresh or frozen blueberries,** divided
I cup	**water**

Spray an 8-inch springform pan with nonstick cooking spray.

In a large bowl, whisk together the eggs, sugar, butter, ricotta, yogurt, zest, and vanilla. In a separate bowl, mix together the flour, cornmeal, salt, and baking powder. Stir dry ingredients into wet ingredients a little at a time, until batter is smooth. Carefully fold in ¾ cup of the blueberries. Pour batter into pan and sprinkle remaining blueberries over top. Cover pan loosely with aluminum foil.

Pour water into Instant Pot® and place the pan on a wire trivet; lower into the pot. Place lid on pot and lock into place to seal. Press the Cake setting or cook on High Pressure for 50 minutes. Let sit for I0 minutes. Use Quick Pressure Release. Let sit for I0 minutes on the counter before releasing the edge of the springform pan. Cut into wedges to serve. Makes 4–6 servings.

SOUPS AND STEWS

HAM AND 15 BEAN SOUP

1 package (20 ounces)	**15 Bean Soup**® with seasoning packet
8 cups	**water**
1	**onion,** diced
2 cloves	**garlic,** minced
2	**bay leaves**
1 teaspoon	**dried thyme leaves**
4 cups	**vegetable stock**
1 tablespoon	**hot sauce**
16 ounces	**diced ham**
1	**ham bone or ham hock,** optional
2 tablespoons	**Worcestershire sauce**
1/4 cup	**ketchup**
	salt and pepper, to taste

Rinse beans and place in a large bowl along with the water; let soak at least 12 hours or overnight. Drain soaking water and rinse beans. Place the beans, contents of seasoning packet, and remaining ingredients except the Worcestershire sauce, ketchup, salt and pepper in the Instant Pot®; stir to combine.

Place lid on pot and lock into place to seal. Cook on High Pressure for 40 minutes. Use Natural Pressure Release. Remove bay leaves and ham bone or hock, if using; pick off any bits of ham and stir back into the soup. Stir in Worcestershire sauce and ketchup. Season with salt and pepper. Makes 6–8 servings.

BACON CORN CHOWDER

4 slices	**bacon,** diced
1	**onion,** diced
4	**red potatoes,** cubed
1 package (16 ounces)	**frozen corn kernels**
3 cups	**water**
1 teaspoon	**dried thyme**
1 pinch	**cayenne pepper**
	salt and pepper, to taste
¾ cup	**heavy cream**
3 tablespoons	**flour**
2 tablespoons	**chopped fresh chives,** optional

Turn Instant Pot® to High Sauté and let heat for about 1 minute. Add the bacon and cook until brown and crispy, about 5 minutes. Add onion and cook, stirring frequently, until onions become translucent, 2–3 minutes. Stir in potatoes, corn, water, thyme, and cayenne; season with salt and pepper. Place lid on pot and lock into place to seal. Cook on High Pressure for 10 minutes. Use Quick Pressure Release. Press Cancel. Empty pot into a large serving bowl; taste and adjust seasoning, if necessary.

Turn pot to Normal Sauté and stir in the cream and flour; cook, whisking frequently, until smooth and slightly thickened, 4–5 minutes. Stir thickened cream into soup. Serve, garnished with chives, if desired. Makes 4–6 servings.

CHICKEN TORTILLA SOUP

2 tablespoons	**vegetable oil**
I pound	**boneless, skinless chicken breasts,** cut into ½-inch chunks
I can (15 ounces)	**fire-roasted diced tomatoes**
I can (10 ounces)	**red enchilada sauce**
3 cloves	**garlic,** minced
I	**yellow onion,** diced
I can (4 ounces)	**fire-roasted diced green chiles**
I can (15 ounces)	**black beans,** drained and rinsed
I cup	**frozen corn kernels**
4 cups	**chicken stock**
I teaspoon	**ground cumin**
2 teaspoons	**chili powder**
	salt and pepper, to taste
	garnishes, of choice, such as chopped cilantro, tortilla strips, lime juice, grated cheese, or diced avocados

Turn Instant Pot® to Normal Sauté. Add the oil and let heat for 1–2 minutes. Add chicken to the pot; stir and cook until lightly browned on both sides. Press Cancel. Add remaining ingredients except salt and pepper and garnishes. Stir, scraping up any browned bits from bottom of pot.

Place lid on pot and lock into place to seal. Cook on High Pressure for 8 minutes. Let sit for 10 minutes. Use Quick Pressure Release. Serve topped with garnishes, as desired. Makes 4–6 servings.

LOADED BAKED POTATO SOUP

1 cup	**water**
1 1/2 pounds	**whole russet potatoes,** peeled
1/4 cup	**butter**
1/4 cup	**flour**
3/4 teaspoon	**salt,** plus extra
1/2 teaspoon	**pepper,** plus extra
4 cups	**milk**
1/2 cup	**sour cream**
1/2 cup	**grated medium or sharp cheddar cheese**
3	**green onions,** thinly sliced
3 ounces	**Real Bacon Bits**
	salt and pepper, to taste

Pour water in the Instant Pot® and lower wire trivet into the bottom. Arrange potatoes on top of the trivet. Place lid on pot and lock into place to seal. Cook on High Pressure for 10 minutes. Use Quick Pressure Release. Press Cancel.

Remove the potatoes and set aside; discard any remaining water. Turn the pot to Normal Sauté and add the butter. Once butter is melted, whisk in the flour 1 tablespoon at a time until you have a smooth and thick roux. Add 3/4 teaspoon salt and 1/2 teaspoon pepper; whisk in milk to combine. Adjust setting to High Sauté, whisking every few minutes until the milk starts to thicken and bubble. Stir in the sour cream, cheese, onions, and bacon bits.

Cut the potatoes into small cubes and smash about 1 cup of the potato cubes. Stir smashed and remaining potatoes cubes into the soup. Season with salt and pepper. Makes 4–6 servings.

FRENCH ONION SOUP

3	**large yellow onions,** peeled
3 tablespoons	**butter**
2 cloves	**garlic,** minced
2 sprigs	**fresh thyme**
1	**bay leaf**
^{1}/$_2$ cup	**water**
^{1}/$_2$ cup	**dry red wine**
4 cups	**beef or vegetable stock**
	salt and pepper, to taste
8–12 (1-inch-thick)	**baguette slices**
4 ounces	**grated Gruyere cheese**

Cut the onions in half pole to pole; and then cut each half into ^{1}/$_4$-inch-thick slices. Turn Instant Pot® to Normal Sauté. Melt the butter and add the onions, garlic, thyme, and bay leaf; stir to combine. Cook, stirring, until onions soften slightly, about 5 minutes; add water. Press Cancel. Place lid on pot and lock into place to seal. Cook on High Pressure for 20 minutes. Use Quick Pressure Release. Press Cancel.

Remove the lid, and press Normal Sauté. Cook for 5 minutes until some of the liquid evaporates; add the wine and bring to a simmer, scraping up browned bits from the bottom. Let simmer for 5–8 minutes, or until most of the wine has evaporated. Discard the thyme and bay leaf. Add the stock and bring to a simmer until the soup thickens. Season with salt and pepper.

Preheat oven broiler. Arrange the baguette slices on a baking sheet in a single layer and sprinkle with cheese. Broil until bubbly and golden brown, 2–3 minutes. Ladle the soup into bowls, and float the bread on top of each serving, cheese side up. Makes 4–6 servings.

WHITE CHICKEN CHILI

2 tablespoons	**vegetable oil,** divided
1	**medium onion,** diced
1	**poblano* pepper,** seeds and ribs removed, diced
1 teaspoon	**salt,** divided
2 teaspoons	**ground cumin**
2 teaspoons	**dried oregano leaves**
3 cloves	**garlic,** minced
2	**boneless, skinless chicken breasts,** cut into bite-size pieces
1 can (14 ounces)	**chicken stock**
1 tablespoon	**cayenne pepper sauce**
2 cans (14 ounces each)	**white beans,** such as navy or cannellini, drained and rinsed
	garnishes of choice, such as chopped fresh cilantro, grated cheese, sliced green onions, optional

Turn Instant Pot® to Normal Sauté. Add 1 tablespoon oil and let heat for 1–2 minutes. Add the onion and cook, stirring occasionally for about 3 minutes, until slightly softened. Add the poblano, ½ teaspoon salt, cumin, oregano, and garlic; cook for 1 minute. Empty contents of pot into a small bowl and set aside.

Add 1 tablespoon oil, ½ teaspoon salt, and chicken to the pot. Cook for about 3 minutes, stirring occasionally until chicken pieces are lightly browned. Add the onion mixture back to the pot along with the stock and pepper sauce. Press Cancel. Place lid on pot and lock into place to seal. Cook for 20 minutes on Low Pressure. Use Quick Pressure Release. Stir beans into pot. Serve garnished, as desired. Makes 4–6 servings.

*Note: If you like more heat, substitute with 1–2 jalapeno peppers.

MINESTRONE IN MINUTES

2 tablespoons	**olive oil**
1	**large carrot,** peeled and diced
3	**small onions,** diced
3 cloves	**garlic,** minced
2 stalks	**celery,** diced
1 can (15 ounces)	**green beans,** drained
1 can (15 ounces)	**kidney beans,** drained and rinsed
1 tablespoon	**Italian seasoning**
6 cups	**vegetable stock**
1 can (28 ounces)	**crushed tomatoes**
1 can (6 ounces)	**tomato paste**
1 cup	**uncooked macaroni**

Turn Instant Pot® to Normal Sauté. Add the oil and let heat for about 1 minute. Add carrots; cook and stir until lightly browned, about 3 minutes. Add onions, garlic, and celery and cook for another 3 minutes, stirring frequently until all vegetables are slightly softened but still firm. Press Cancel.

Stir in remaining ingredients except macaroni. Place lid on pot and lock into place to seal. Cook on High Pressure for 5 minutes. Use Quick Pressure Release. Stir macaroni into soup and replace lid. Leave macaroni to sit and soak up some of the soup's liquid, about 10 minutes. Test macaroni to see if it is done. If not, let sit with lid on for a few more minutes until done to your liking. Makes 6–8 servings.

QUICK CLAM CHOWDER

2 cans (6 ounces each)	**chopped clams,** drained, juice reserved
4 slices	**bacon,** diced
3 tablespoons	**butter**
I	**medium onion,** diced
2 stalks	**celery,** diced
I tablespoon	**cornstarch**
I $\frac{1}{2}$ pounds	**russet potatoes,** peeled and cut into $\frac{1}{2}$-inch chunks
I $\frac{1}{2}$ cups	**half-and-half**
	chopped fresh chives, optional
	salt and pepper, to taste

Place reserved clam juice in a large measuring cup and add enough water to make 2 cups of liquid. Set aside.

Turn Instant Pot® to Normal Sauté and let heat for I−2 minutes. Add the bacon and cook, stirring occasionally, until fat has rendered out. Add the butter, onion, and celery. Cook, stirring and scraping the bottom of the pot to get up all of the browned bits, until the onion starts turning translucent; stir in the cornstarch. Stir in the potatoes and clam juice. Press Cancel. Place lid on pot and lock into place to seal. Cook on High Pressure for 5 minutes. Let sit I0 minutes. Use Quick Pressure Release.

Chop the clams into smaller pieces, if desired, and stir into soup. Use a potato masher to carefully mash some or all of the potato chunks. Stir in half-and-half and season with salt and pepper. Ladle into bowls and garnish with chives, if desired. Makes 4−6 servings.

CHICKEN NOODLE SOUP

2 tablespoons	**butter**
2	**boneless, skinless chicken breasts,** cut into bite-size pieces
	salt and pepper, to taste
I tablespoon	**cornstarch**
4 cups	**chicken stock**
4 cups	**water**
8 ounces	**frozen mixed vegetables**
6 ounces	**wide egg noodles**

Set Instant Pot® to Normal Sauté and let heat for about I minute. Add the butter and let melt. Add the chicken and season with salt and pepper. Stir occasionally and let brown, 5–8 minutes. Stir in cornstarch and cook for I minute. Add stock, water, vegetables, and noodles; stir.

Place lid on top of pot and lock into place to seal. Cook on High Pressure for I2 minutes. Let sit I0 minutes. Use Quick Pressure Release. Makes 4–6 servings.

LENTILS AND SAUSAGE STEW

1 tablespoon	**vegetable oil**
14 ounces	**kielbasa-style sausage,** cut into 1/2-inch-thick slices
1 1/2 cups	**green lentils,** rinsed and picked through
4 cups	**vegetable or beef stock**
1/2	**large sweet onion,** diced
1 can (15 ounces)	**diced tomatoes,** with liquid
2 tablespoons	**soy sauce**
1 tablespoon	**Dijon mustard**
2 tablespoons	**brown sugar**
2 tablespoons	**Worcestershire sauce or steak sauce**
1 tablespoon	**cayenne pepper sauce**
	salt and pepper, to taste

Turn Instant Pot® to Normal Sauté. Add oil and let heat for about 1 minute. Add sausage and cook until lightly browned on both sides, stirring occasionally. Add remaining ingredients and stir to combine. Press Cancel.

Place lid on pot and lock into place to seal. Cook on High Pressure for 25 minutes. Use Quick Pressure Release. Taste and adjust seasoning, if necessary. Makes 4–6 servings.

MIRACLE BEEF STEW

3 tablespoons	**vegetable oil,** divided
2 pounds	**beef chuck roast,** visible fat removed, cut into bite-size chunks
I	**large russet potato,** cut into 2-inch chunks
2	**carrots,** peeled and sliced into $1/2$-inch-thick chunks
2 stalks	**celery,** cut in $1/2$-inch-thick slices
I $1/2$ cups	**beef stock**
2 tablespoons	**steak or Worcestershire sauce**
2 tablespoons	**tomato paste**
2 tablespoons	**cornstarch mixed with 2 tablespoons water**

Turn Instant Pot® to High Sauté. Add I tablespoon of oil and let heat for about I minute. Add half of the beef and cook until lightly browned on all sides. Remove beef to a plate; reserve. Repeat process with remaining beef.

Add remaining I tablespoon oil to pot. Stir in the reserved cooked beef, potato, carrots, and celery. In a small bowl, whisk together the stock, steak sauce, and tomato paste, to combine; add to the pot and stir. Press Cancel.

Place lid on pot and lock into place to seal. Cook on High Pressure for 30 minutes. Let sit for 10 minutes. Use Quick Pressure Release. Turn to Normal Sauté. Stir in cornstarch mixture and cook for 1–2 minutes, or until thickened. Makes 4–6 servings.

KITCHEN SINK SOUP

2 tablespoons	**olive oil**
½ cup	**diced ham or bacon** (omit for vegetarian)
1 cup	**diced onion**
1 cup	**diced root vegetables,** such as potatoes, carrots, and/or celery
3 cups	**diced vine vegetables,** such as yellow squash, corn, and/or tomatoes
1 cup	**uncooked rice**
8 cups	**vegetable stock**
2 tablespoons	**tomato paste**
2 tablespoons	**soy sauce**
4 cups	**loosely packed chopped greens,** such as spinach, kale, or chard

Set Instant Pot® to Normal Sauté. Add the oil and let heat for 1–2 minutes. Add the ham or bacon, if using, onion, and root vegetables; stir and cook for a few minutes, until vegetables are slightly softened. Stir in remaining vegetables and rice.

In a large bowl, whisk together the stock, tomato paste, and soy sauce. Add to the pot and stir. Press Cancel. Place lid on pot and lock into place to seal. Cook on High Pressure for 10 minutes. Use Quick Pressure Release.

Place greens on top of mixture in pot; do not stir. Replace lid and lock into place to seal. Press Keep Warm and let sit for 10 minutes, or until greens are wilted. Stir to combine before serving. Makes 6–8 servings.

KALE, SAUSAGE, AND WHITE BEAN SOUP

1 tablespoon	**vegetable oil**
8 ounces	**cooked sweet Italian sausage,** without casings
4 cups	**chopped kale**
4 cups	**low sodium chicken stock**
2 cans (15 ounces each)	**white cannellini beans,** drained and rinsed
2 ounces	**grated Parmesan cheese**

Turn Instant Pot® to Normal Sauté. Add the oil and let heat for 1–2 minutes. Add the sausage and kale, and cook, breaking sausage into small crumbles, until lightly browned, about 3 minutes. Add stock and beans; stir.

Place lid on pot and lock into place to seal. Cook on High Pressure for 3 minutes. Use Quick Pressure Release. Garnish with Parmesan, to serve. Makes 4–6 servings.

BROCCOLI CHEDDAR SOUP

2 tablespoons	**butter**
1/2	**large onion,** diced
3 cloves	**garlic,** minced
4 cups	**fresh or frozen and thawed chopped broccoli**
2 cups	**vegetable stock**
1 cup	**sour cream**
2 cups	**grated sharp cheddar cheese** **salt and pepper,** to taste

Turn Instant Pot® to High Sauté and heat for 1–2 minutes. Add the butter and the onion. Stir and cook for 3–5 minutes until onion is softened and lightly browned around the edges. Add garlic and cook for 1 minute. Stir in broccoli and stock. Press Cancel.

Place lid on pot and lock into place to seal. Cook on High Pressure for 5 minutes. Let sit for 10 minutes. Use Quick Pressure Release.

Scoop out the vegetables using a strainer or large slotted spoon and place in a food processor or blender and puree; stir back into pot. Add sour cream and cheese, stirring until completely melted. Season with salt and pepper. Makes 4–6 servings.

BEEF AND PORK

BEEF STROGANOFF

2 tablespoons	**vegetable oil**
2 pounds	**beef chuck roast,** visible fat removed
	salt and pepper, to taste
8 ounces	**cremini mushrooms**
1	**yellow onion,** peeled
2 tablespoons	**butter**
1 tablespoon	**minced garlic**
2 cups	**beef stock,** divided
2 tablespoons	**flour**
2 tablespoons	**Worcestershire sauce**
1/2 cup	**sour cream**
1 package (12 ounces)	**egg noodles,** cooked and kept warm
	chopped fresh parsley

Turn Instant Pot® to Normal Sauté. Add the oil and let heat for 1–2 minutes. Season both sides of the roast generously with salt and pepper. Add roast to the pot and sear on both sides until well-browned, 4–5 minutes per side. Remove beef to a plate and set aside to rest.

Cut the mushrooms and onion into 1/4-inch-thick slices and add to the pot along with the butter. Cook for 3–5 minutes, or until mushrooms are lightly browned and onions are softened. Add garlic and cook for 1 minute. Pour 1/2 cup stock into the pot, scraping up browned bits from the bottom.

Cut the roast against the grain into thin strips, about 1/4-inch thick. Place in a large bowl, sprinkle the flour over top, and toss to coat. Add to the pot along with remaining stock and Worcestershire sauce. Place lid on pot and lock into place to seal. Cook on High Pressure for 12 minutes. Let sit for 10 minutes. Use Quick Pressure Release. Press Cancel.

Turn pot to Normal Sauté. Stir in the sour cream and cook until sauce is thickened as desired. Taste and adjust seasoning, if needed. Serve over warm noodles, and garnish with parsley. Makes 4–6 servings.

RED BEANS AND RICE

1 pound	**dried kidney beans,** rinsed and sorted through
1 teaspoon	**salt**
2–3 tablespoons	**hot sauce**
2 teaspoons	**dried thyme leaves**
6 cups	**water**
1	**medium onion,** diced
1	**bell pepper,** diced
3 stalks	**celery,** cut into $^1/_2$-inch-thick slices
8 ounces	**cooked Andouille sausage,** cut into $^1/_4$-inch-thick half-moon slices
$^1/_4$ cup	**ketchup**
8 cups	**hot cooked rice**

Add beans, salt, hot sauce, thyme, and water to Instant Pot®. Place lid on pot and lock into place to seal. Cook on High Pressure for 25 minutes. Use Quick Pressure Release.

Stir in the onion, bell pepper, celery, and sausage. Replace lid and lock into place to seal. Cook on High Pressure for 10 minutes. Let sit for 10 minutes. Use Quick Pressure Release. Press Cancel. Stir in ketchup. Serve over rice. Makes 6–8 servings.

SWEET AND SPICY
BEEF WITH BROCCOLI

2 tablespoons	**vegetable oil**
I pound	**flank steak,** cut across the grain in $\frac{1}{4}$-inch-thick strips
$\frac{1}{2}$ cup	**brown sugar**
4 cloves	**garlic,** minced
I tablespoon	**minced fresh gingerroot**
$\frac{1}{2}$ cup	**low-sodium soy sauce**
I cup	**water**
I teaspoon	**red pepper flakes**
4 cups	**broccoli florets,** cut into bite-size pieces
2 tablespoons	**cornstarch mixed with $\frac{1}{4}$ cup water**
6 cups	**hot cooked rice**
	sliced green onions
	sesame seeds

Turn Instant Pot® to Normal Sauté. Add the oil and let heat for I–2 minutes. Add the beef and cook for 2–3 minutes, stirring occasionally, until browned. Add the sugar, garlic, ginger, soy sauce, water, and pepper flakes. Stir well to combine, making sure beef strips are coated with sauce. Scatter broccoli on top of beef mixture. Do not stir. Place lid on pot and lock into place to seal. Cook on High Pressure for 8 minutes. Let sit 10 minutes. Use Quick Pressure Release. Press Cancel.

Turn to Normal Sauté. Stir the cornstarch mixture into the pot and cook for 2–3 minutes, stirring occasionally, until the sauce thickens. Press Cancel and let sit for 10 minutes. Serve over rice, garnished with green onions and sesame seeds, as desired. Makes 4–6 servings.

UNSTUFFED CABBAGE CASSEROLE

I pound	**lean ground beef**
2 teaspoons	**salt**
I teaspoon	**pepper**
I	**small onion,** diced
½	**green bell pepper,** diced
I can (28 ounces)	**diced tomatoes,** with liquid
I can (8 ounces)	**tomato sauce**
3 tablespoons	**brown sugar**
3 tablespoons	**apple cider vinegar**
2 tablespoons	**Worcestershire sauce or steak sauce**
2 teaspoons	**Italian seasoning**
I cup	**uncooked long-grain white rice**
2 cups	**water**
½	**large cabbage**

Turn Instant Pot® to High Sauté and let heat for about I minute. Add beef and cook for about 3 minutes, stirring and breaking up into small bits. Add the salt, pepper, onion, and bell pepper; continue to stir and cook until vegetables are slightly softened.

In a large bowl, whisk together the tomatoes and liquid, tomato sauce, sugar, vinegar, Worcestershire sauce, and seasoning. Stir into beef mixture. Stir in rice and water. Cut cabbage into quarters, removing the center core. Cut quarters into ½-inch-thick slices and place on top of the beef mixture; do not stir together. Press Cancel.

Place lid on pot and lock into place to seal. Cook on High Pressure for 20 minutes. Let sit for I0 minutes. Use Quick Pressure Release. Stir contents together, to serve. Makes 6–8 servings.

SMOKY MAPLE BRISKET

2 tablespoons	**maple syrup**
2 tablespoons	**Dijon mustard**
2 tablespoons	**liquid smoke**
1 1/2 pounds	**beef brisket**
2 tablespoons	**smoked paprika**
1 tablespoon	**ground cumin**
2 teaspoons	**salt**
2 tablespoons	**vegetable oil**
1 cup	**beef or vegetable stock**
1/4 cup	**cornstarch mixed with 1/2 cup water**

In a small bowl, whisk together the syrup, mustard, and liquid smoke. Brush evenly over both sides of the brisket. In another small bowl, mix together the paprika, cumin, and salt; sprinkle evenly over both sides of the brisket.

Turn Instant Pot® to High Sauté. Add the oil and let heat for 1–2 minutes. Place brisket in pot and cook for 3–5 minutes on each side, until well-browned. Press Cancel. Add the stock. Place lid on pot and lock into place to seal. Cook on High Pressure for 50 minutes. Let pressure release naturally for at least 20 minutes. Press Cancel. Remove brisket to a serving platter and let rest.

Turn pot to High Sauté. Whisk cornstarch mixture into pot and cook for 2–3 minutes, stirring, until gravy is thickened. Serve brisket sliced thinly with gravy drizzled on top. Makes 4–6 servings.

PERFECT POT ROAST DINNER

2 tablespoons	**vegetable oil**
	salt and pepper, to taste
2 pounds	**boneless beef chuck roast,** visible fat removed
1 cup	**beef or vegetable stock**
2 tablespoons	**ketchup**
2 tablespoons	**Worcestershire sauce or steak sauce**
2 cups	**baby carrots**
3 stalks	**celery,** cut into 1-inch chunks
1	**large sweet onion,** peeled and cut into 8 wedges
2 cups	**baby red potatoes,** about 2 inches in diameter
3 tablespoons	**cornstarch**
3 tablespoons	**soy sauce**

Turn Instant Pot® to Normal Sauté. Add the oil and let heat for 1–2 minutes. Season both sides of roast generously with salt and pepper and place in the pot. Let cook until well browned, about 5 minutes. Turn roast over and press Cancel.

In a small bowl, stir together the stock, ketchup, and Worcestershire sauce; pour evenly over the roast. Add the carrots, celery, onion, and potatoes. Place lid on pot and lock into place to seal. Cook on High Pressure for 50 minutes. Use Quick Pressure Release.

Remove all the vegetables to a bowl and the roast to a serving platter, leaving juices in the pot. Turn pot to Normal Sauté. In a small cup whisk together the cornstarch and soy sauce until smooth, and then whisk into the pot. Cook until gravy thickens, 3–5 minutes. Press Cancel. Stir the vegetables back into the pot and cut the roast into large chunks. To serve, ladle vegetables with gravy over top of roast. Makes 4–6 servings.

CORNED BEEF AND CABBAGE

3 pounds	**corned beef brisket,** with seasoning packet
2 cups	**water**
2 cups	**baby carrots**
1 pound	**small Red Bliss potatoes**
1	**small green cabbage**

Place brisket in Instant Pot® and sprinkle seasoning packet over top; add the water. Place lid on pot and lock into place to seal. Cook on High Pressure for 60 minutes. Use Quick Pressure Release. Remove brisket to a serving platter, leaving juices in the pot.

Add the carrots and potatoes to the pot, cutting any large potatoes in half. Cut cabbage into quarters, removing the core. Cut each quarter in half and place in pot. (Cabbage will be above the liquid in the pot.) Replace lid and lock into place to seal. Cook on High Pressure for 8 minutes. Use Quick Pressure Release.

Cut brisket into 1/2-inch-thick slices and spoon vegetables over top to serve. Makes 6–8 servings.

SOUTHWEST SHREDDED BEEF

2 tablespoons	**vegetable oil**
3 pounds	**beef chuck roast,** visible fat removed
3 tablespoons	**southwest spice blend***
I tablespoon	**salt**
I cup	**beef stock**

Turn Instant Pot® to Normal Sauté. Add the oil and let heat for I–2 minutes. Add the roast and cook for 3–4 minutes on each side, or until completely browned. Mix the spice blend and salt together and sprinkle evenly over top of roast. Pour stock around the edges of the roast.

Place lid on pot and lock into place to seal. Cook on High Pressure for 60 minutes. Press Cancel and let pressure release naturally. Remove the roast to a large plate and let it rest.

Turn pot to Normal Sauté. Bring the remaining juices in the pot to a simmer, whisking occasionally until reduced in half, about 5 minutes. Shred the meat and return to the pot; stir. Press the Keep Warm setting until ready to serve. Great for use in casseroles, enchiladas, tacos, or served over rice. Makes 4 cups.

*Note: To make your own southwest spice blend, in a small bowl, mix together 2 tablespoons chili powder, 2 teaspoons ground cumin, and I teaspoon garlic powder.

EGG ROLL BOWLS

3 tablespoons	**vegetable oil,** divided
16 ounces	**ground pork**
1/2 cup	**vegetable or chicken stock**
3 tablespoons	**soy sauce,** or to taste
1 tablespoon	**ground ginger**
1 tablespoon	**garlic powder**
1 tablespoon	**cayenne pepper sauce**
1 bag (16 ounces)	**shredded coleslaw mix**
12 (4-inch square)	**wonton wrappers,** optional

Turn Instant Pot® to High Sauté. Add 1 tablespoon oil and let heat for 1–2 minutes. Add the pork and cook until browned, breaking up into small bits. Press Cancel and stir in the stock, scraping up browned bits from the bottom of the pot. Stir in soy sauce, ginger, garlic powder, and pepper sauce.

Place coleslaw mix on top; do not stir. Place lid on pot and lock into place to seal. Cook on Normal Pressure for 2 minutes. Use Quick Pressure Release, and stir everything together.

Preheat oven broiler.

If desired, you can make wonton chips by cutting each wrapper into 2 triangles. Place on a baking sheet and lightly brush both sides of the triangles with remaining 2 tablespoons of oil. Broil for 1–2 minutes, until lightly browned; turn triangles over and broil for about 1 minute, or until lightly browned. Top each serving with a garnish of wonton chips. Makes 4–6 servings.

COLA MARINATED RIBS

2 pounds	**baby back pork ribs**
2 tablespoons	**salt**
4 cups	**regular cola** (not diet)
1 cup	**water**
1 cup	**barbecue sauce,** of choice

Place ribs in a gallon size ziplock bag. Add salt and cola; seal the bag and turn a few times to coat ribs. Refrigerate for 12–24 hours.

Place wire trivet in Instant Pot® and add the water. Remove ribs from marinade and arrange on the trivet. Place lid on pot and lock into place to seal. Cook on High Pressure for 40 minutes. Allow pressure to release naturally for 10 minutes. Use Quick Pressure Release.

Preheat oven broiler.

Place ribs on a baking sheet and brush barbecue sauce over ribs, covering completely. Broil at top of oven until the barbecue sauce begins to bubble, about 3 minutes. Turn ribs over and broil other side until sauce is bubbly and browned. Makes 4–6 servings.

ROOT BEER PULLED PORK

2 tablespoons	**vegetable oil**
3–4 pounds	**bone-in pork shoulder roast,** visible fat removed
1 teaspoon	**salt**
½ cup	**good quality regular root beer**
1 cup	**barbecue sauce,** of choice, divided

Turn Instant Pot® to Normal Sauté. Add the oil and let heat for 1–2 minutes. Cut roast into 2 large pieces and add to the pot; let cook for about 3 minutes on each side until browned. Press Cancel.

In a small bowl, whisk together the salt, root beer, and ½ cup barbecue sauce; pour evenly over the roast. Place lid on pot and lock into place to seal. Cook on High Pressure for 45 minutes. Let sit for 10 minutes. Use Quick Pressure Release. Remove meat from the pot and place on a large cutting board; let cool to warm.

Turn pot to High Sauté, and simmer the juices for 10–12 minutes, whisking frequently until thickened and reduced to about 1 cup of sauce. Stir remaining 1/2 cup barbecue sauce into the pot. Shred the meat and place back into the pot; tossing to coat with the sauce. Serve on buns or as a main dish. Makes 6–8 servings.

SPEEDY SPAGHETTI

2 tablespoons	**vegetable oil**
8 ounces	**Italian sausage,** casings removed
1/2	**onion,** diced
3 cloves	**garlic,** minced
1 jar (24 ounces)	**marinara sauce**
2 cups	**water**
8 ounces	**spaghetti noodles**
	toppings of choice, such as sliced olives, chopped parsley, or freshly grated Parmesan cheese, optional

Turn Instant Pot® to Normal Sauté. Add oil and let heat for 1–2 minutes. Add the sausage and cook until browned, breaking into crumbles. Stir in the onion and cook until softened, about 3 minutes. Stir in garlic and cook for 1 minute. Add marinara and water; stir and bring to a simmer.

Break spaghetti noodles in half, add to the pot, and stir to separate and coat with sauce. Press Cancel. Place lid on pot and lock into place to seal. Cook on High Pressure for 10 minutes. Use Quick Pressure Release. Makes 4–6 servings.

SMOTHERED PORK CHOPS

4 (4–6 ounces each)	**center cut blade pork chops**
2 tablespoons	**smoked paprika**
2 tablespoons	**garlic powder**
2 teaspoons	**salt**
1 teaspoon	**pepper**
2 tablespoons	**vegetable oil**
1/2 cup	**vegetable stock**
1	**medium onion**
8 ounces	**cremini mushrooms,** cut into 1/4-inch-thick slices
2 tablespoons	**cornstarch mixed with 2 tablespoons water**
1/2 cup	**sour cream**

Lay chops on a flat surface. In a small bowl, mix together the paprika, garlic powder, salt, and pepper. Sprinkle spice mixture evenly on both sides of each pork chop. Turn Instant Pot® to High Sauté, add oil and let heat for 1–2 minutes. Add 2 of the chops and cook for about 3 minutes on each side, until browned. Remove chops to a plate and set aside. Repeat with remaining chops. Press Cancel.

Add stock to the pot scraping up brown bits from the bottom. Peel and cut onion in half from pole to pole, and cut each half into 1/2-inch-wide slices. Add onion and mushrooms to the pot; set pork chops on top. Place lid on pot and lock into place to seal. Cook on High Pressure for 20 minutes. Use Quick Pressure Release. Remove pork chops and vegetables to a platter. Press Cancel.

Turn pot to High Sauté and bring remaining cooking juices to a simmer. Continue simmering for about 5 minutes, until slightly reduced. Whisk in the cornstarch mixture and cook until thickened. Press Cancel. Whisk in sour cream. Ladle gravy over the pork and vegetables, to serve. Makes 4 servings.

JAMMIN' JAMBALAYA

I tablespoon	**vegetable oil**
12 ounces	**andouille or spicy kielbasa sausage,** sliced into ¼-inch half moons
2	**boneless, skinless chicken thighs,** cut into 1-inch chunks
1 cup	**diced onion**
1 cup	**diced bell pepper**
1 cup	**½ inch-thick celery slices**
3 cloves	**garlic,** minced
I tablespoon	**Cajun seasoning or chili powder**
1 ½ cups	**uncooked long-grain white rice**
I can (15 ounces)	**diced tomatoes,** with liquid
2 cups	**vegetable stock**
I tablespoon	**cayenne pepper sauce**

Turn Instant Pot® to High Sauté. Add the oil and let heat for 1–2 minutes. Add the sausage and cook until lightly browned. Remove sausage to a plate; set aside. Add chicken to the pot and cook until browned on all sides. Remove chicken to the plate with the sausage, leaving rendered fat and oil in the pot. Add onion, bell pepper, and celery; stir and cook until slightly softened, about 2 minutes. Add garlic and cook for 1 minute.

Return the sausage and chicken to the pot. Stir in seasoning, rice, tomatoes and liquid, stock, and pepper sauce. Press Cancel. Place lid on pot and lock into place to seal. Cook on High Pressure for 8 minutes. Use Quick Pressure Release. Makes 4–6 servings.

POULTRY

APRICOT PINEAPPLE CHICKEN THIGHS

2 tablespoons	**vegetable oil**
6	**chicken thighs,** skin and visible fat removed
1/2 cup	**apricot pineapple jam**
1 tablespoon	**soy sauce**
1 cup	**water**

Turn Instant Pot® to High Sauté; add the oil and let heat for 1–2 minutes. Add 3 of the chicken thighs to the pot and cook until golden brown on each side, about 3 minutes. Remove to a plate and set aside. Repeat with remaining thighs. Press Cancel.

In a medium bowl, whisk together the jam and soy sauce; add the chicken thighs and toss until well coated. Pour water into the pot. Place the wire trivet in the pot and arrange thighs on top of trivet. Press Cancel. Place lid on pot and lock into place to seal. Cook on High Pressure for 20 minutes. Let sit for 10 minutes. Use Quick Pressure Release. Press Cancel.

Remove thighs to a serving plate. Turn pot to High Sauté and bring remaining cooking juices to a simmer until starting to thicken, about 5 minutes; whisk frequently. Drizzle sauce over chicken, to serve. Makes 6 servings.

WHOLE ROASTED CHICKEN WITH VEGETABLES

I	**medium onion,** coarsely chopped
2	**large carrots,** peeled and coarsely chopped
3 stalks	**celery,** coarsely chopped
8 cloves	**garlic,** peeled
2 cups	**water**
2 tablespoons	**butter,** at room temperature
I teaspoon	**seasoned salt**
I (5 pound)	**whole chicken**
2 tablespoons	**cornstarch mixed with $\frac{1}{4}$ cup water**

Place the onion, carrots, celery, and garlic into the Instant Pot® and add the water. Mix the butter and seasoned salt together and then spread evenly under the skin on top of chicken breast using your fingers. Set the chicken into the pot on top of the vegetables. Place lid on pot and lock into place to seal. Cook on High Pressure for 25 minutes. Press Cancel and let sit for 15 minutes. Use Quick Pressure Release.

Remove chicken and vegetables to a serving platter, leaving juices in the pot. Turn to Normal Sauté. Whisk in the cornstarch mixture and cook until gravy is thickened, about 5 minutes. Drizzle gravy over chicken and vegetables, to serve. Makes 4–6 servings.

HULI HULI CHICKEN

4	**boneless, skinless chicken breasts**
1/3 cup	**vegetable or chicken stock**
1/2 cup	**pineapple juice**
1/4 cup	**soy sauce**
1/2 cup	**brown sugar**
3 tablespoons	**tomato paste**
1 tablespoon	**grated fresh gingerroot**
3 cloves	**garlic,** minced
2 tablespoons	**cornstarch mixed with 1/4 cup water**
6 cups	**hot cooked rice**
	sliced green onions
	diced pineapple

Cut chicken into 2-inch chunks and place in Instant Pot®. Stir in the stock, pineapple juice, soy sauce, sugar, tomato paste, ginger, and garlic. Place lid on pot and lock into place to seal. Cook at High Pressure for 15 minutes. Use Quick Pressure Release. Press Cancel.

Turn to Normal Sauté. Stir cornstarch mixture into pot and cook until sauce is thickened. Smash chicken pieces lightly with a potato masher. Serve over rice, garnished with onions and pineapple, as desired. Makes 4–6 servings.

HONEY GARLIC CHICKEN

4	**chicken thighs,** skin and visible fat removed
	salt and pepper, to taste
I tablespoon	**vegetable oil,** divided
4 cloves	**garlic,** minced
3 tablespoons	**honey**
2 tablespoons	**soy sauce**
½ cup	**chicken stock**
3 dashes	**cayenne pepper sauce**

Season the chicken thighs with salt and pepper; set aside. Turn Instant Pot® to Normal Sauté. Add ½ tablespoon oil and let heat for about I minute. Add the thighs and cook for about 3 minutes on each side, or until golden brown. Remove thighs to a plate and set aside.

Add the remaining ½ tablespoon oil and garlic to the pot and cook, stirring, for about I minute. Add the honey, soy sauce, stock, and pepper sauce; stir to combine. Return thighs to the pot; toss to coat with the sauce. Place lid on pot and lock into place to seal. Cook on High Pressure for I0 minutes. Let sit for 20 minutes. Use Quick Pressure Release. Remove chicken and place on a serving plate. Turn pot to High Sauté and reduce liquid until it is very thick. Brush on both sides of chicken before serving. Makes 4 servings.

CHICKEN CORDON BLEU PASTA

16 ounces	**penne pasta**
3 1/2 cups	**chicken stock**
16 ounces	**boneless, skinless chicken breast**
16 ounces	**sliced ham**
4 ounces	**grated Gouda cheese**
4 ounces	**grated Swiss cheese**
8 ounces	**cream,** heated
2 tablespoons	**cream cheese,** at room temperature
3 tablespoons	**Dijon mustard**
2 tablespoons	**butter**
1/4 cup	**Panko-style breadcrumbs**

Add pasta to Instant Pot® and pour in stock; stir. Cut chicken and ham slices into 1/4-inch-wide pieces and scatter over the stock; do not stir. Place lid on pot and lock into place to seal. Cook for 8 minutes on High Pressure. Use Quick Pressure Release. Press Cancel.

Stir in the Gouda and Swiss cheese, until melted. In a small bowl, whisk together the cream, cream cheese, and mustard until well-combined; stir into pot. Empty contents of pot into a large serving bowl and wipe out the pot. Turn to Normal Sauté. Add the butter and breadcrumbs; stir and cook until lightly browned. Sprinkle buttered breadcrumbs over pasta, to serve. Makes 6 servings.

HERB BUTTER TURKEY BREAST

4 tablespoons	**butter,** at room temperature
1 tablespoon	**dried parsley flakes**
½ teaspoon	**dried sage leaves**
1 teaspoon	**dried Italian herbs**
1 (2½–3 pound)	**turkey breast**
½ cup	**lemon juice**
1 tablespoon	**lemon zest**
½ cup	**white wine vinegar**
2 tablespoons	**cornstarch mixed with ¼ cup water**

In a small bowl, mix together the butter, parsley, sage, and Italian herbs. Gently loosen the skin from the turkey breast and rub mixture evenly under the skin and over the top of the breast. Place turkey breast in Instant Pot®. Combine the juice, zest, and vinegar together in a small bowl and pour over turkey breast.

Place lid on pot and lock in to place to seal. Cook on High Pressure for 30 minutes. Let sit for 10 minutes. Use Quick Pressure Release. Press Cancel. Remove turkey breast to a platter. Turn pot to Normal Sauté. Whisk cornstarch mixture into remaining cooking juices and cook, stirring, until gravy is thickened as desired. Carve the turkey breast into ½-inch-thick slices, and ladle gravy over top or serve on the side, as desired. Makes 6–8 servings.

CHICKEN BROCCOLI CASSEROLE

4 tablespoons	**butter,** divided
I	**medium onion,** diced
3 cloves	**garlic,** minced
I pound	**boneless, skinless chicken breasts,** cut into I-inch chunks
2 cups	**chicken stock**
2 cups	**diced broccoli florets**
I cup	**uncooked long-grain white rice**
¼ cup	**grated Parmesan cheese**
I tablespoon	**cayenne pepper sauce**
I cup	**plain Greek yogurt**
	salt and pepper, to taste
I cup	**grated sharp cheddar cheese**

Turn Instant Pot® to High Sauté and let heat for I–2 minutes. Add 2 tablespoons butter and melt. Add onion and cook for about 3 minutes, stirring occasionally, until softened. Add garlic and cook for I minute. Empty the pot into a medium bowl and set aside.

Add remaining 2 tablespoons butter and chicken to the pot. Cook until lightly browned, stirring occasionally, for 3–5 minutes. Stir in stock, broccoli, and rice, scraping up browned bits from bottom of pot. Press Cancel. Place lid on pot and lock into place to seal. Cook on High Pressure for 5 minutes. Let sit for 10 minutes. Use Quick Pressure Release.

Stir in Parmesan, reserved vegetables, pepper sauce, and yogurt. Season with salt and pepper. Sprinkle cheddar cheese over top and let melt. Makes 4–6 servings.

STICKY ASIAN CHICKEN THIGHS

⅓ cup	**honey**
⅓ cup	**ketchup**
2 tablespoons	**low sodium soy sauce**
1 tablespoon	**Sriracha sauce or hot sauce**
3 cloves	**garlic,** minced
3 tablespoons	**vegetable oil**
1 tablespoon	**sesame oil**
6	**skinless chicken thighs**
1 tablespoon	**sesame seeds**
	green onions, thinly sliced

In a small bowl, whisk together the honey, ketchup, soy sauce, Sriracha, and garlic. Set aside.

Turn Instant Pot® to High Sauté. Add the vegetable and sesame oil and let heat for 1–2 minutes. Add 3 of the chicken thighs, and cook for about 3 minutes on each side, or until golden brown. Remove to a plate and set aside. Cook the remaining 3 thighs until golden brown on both sides. Add the reserved thighs back into the pot and pour honey mixture over chicken; toss to coat. Press Cancel.

Place lid on pot and lock into place to seal. Cook on High Pressure for 20 minutes. Let sit for 10 minutes. Use Quick Pressure Release. Remove chicken to a serving plate. Press Cancel. Turn pot to High Sauté and let remaining cooking juices simmer and thicken for about 5 minutes, whisking frequently.

To serve, drizzle sauce over chicken and garnish with sesame seeds and onions. Makes 6 servings.

CHICKEN CURRY IN A HURRY

2 tablespoons	**coconut oil**
4	**boneless, skinless chicken thighs**
I tablespoon	**curry powder**
I can (13.5 ounces)	**coconut milk**
I pound	**fingerling potatoes,** cut into 2-inch chunks
2 cups	**baby carrots,** cut into 1-inch chunks
½	**large onion,** cut into 1-inch chunks
I teaspoon	**salt**
2 tablespoons	**cornstarch mixed with ¼ cup water**
4–6 cups	**hot cooked rice**

Turn Instant Pot® to Normal Sauté. Add oil and let heat for 1–2 minutes. Add chicken thighs and cook for about 3 minutes on each side, or until golden brown. Remove thighs to a cutting board and let sit until cool enough to handle, then cut into bite-size pieces.

Stir curry powder into the pot and cook for 1 minute. Add coconut milk and stir, scraping up browned bits from bottom of pot. Press Cancel. Add the potatoes, carrots, onion, and chicken pieces. Stir in salt. Place lid on pot and lock into place to seal. Cook on High Pressure for 5 minutes. Use Quick Pressure Release. Press Cancel.

Turn pot to Normal Sauté and bring contents to a simmer. Whisk in the cornstarch mixture and cook for 1–2 minutes, or until thickened. Serve over hot rice. Makes 4–6 servings.

PB&J CHICKEN THIGHS

¼ cup	**creamy peanut butter**
¼ cup	**grape jelly**
1 tablespoon	**apple cider vinegar**
1 tablespoon	**hot sauce**
1 teaspoon	**salt**
4	**chicken thighs,** skin and visible fat removed
1 cup	**water**

In a small bowl, whisk together the peanut butter, jelly, vinegar, hot sauce, and salt. Use ¼ cup of the peanut butter sauce to rub over the thighs, making sure to cover completely.

Pour water into Instant Pot®. Crumple up 4 pieces of aluminum foil and place in pot so that the foil sits about 1 inch high above the water. Arrange coated thighs on top of the foil. Place lid on pot and lock into place to seal. Cook on High Pressure for 8 minutes. Let sit 10 minutes. Use Quick Pressure Release.

Preheat oven broiler.

Place thighs on a baking sheet and brush with the remaining sauce. Broil for 4–5 minutes, until sauce is bubbly and thighs are browned in spots. Makes 4 servings.

CHICKEN BURRITO BOWLS

1 tablespoon	**vegetable oil**
1	**small onion,** diced
2 cloves	**garlic,** minced
1 tablespoon	**chili powder**
2 teaspoons	**ground cumin**
½ cup	**chicken stock,** divided
3	**boneless, skinless chicken thighs,** cut into 1-inch pieces
1 can (15 ounces)	**black beans,** drained and rinsed
1 cup	**frozen corn kernels**
1 jar (16 ounces)	**salsa,** of choice
¾ cup	**uncooked long-grain white rice**
½ cup	**grated cheddar cheese**
	garnishes, of choice, such as chopped cilantro, sliced green onions, or diced avocado, optional

Turn Instant Pot® to Normal Sauté. Add oil and let heat for 1–2 minutes. Add the onion and garlic, and cook, stirring occasionally, until softened, 3–4 minutes. Stir in the chili powder and cumin and cook until fragrant, about 30 seconds. Add the stock and cook, scraping up browned bits from bottom of pot; simmer for 1 minute. Press Cancel.

Add the chicken, beans, corn, and salsa; stir to combine. Sprinkle the rice evenly on top of the chicken mixture; do not stir. Place lid on pot and lock into place to seal. Cook on High Pressure for 10 minutes. Let sit 10 minutes. Use Quick Pressure Release. Serve topped with cheese and garnishes, as desired. Makes 4–6 servings.

INDIAN BUTTER CHICKEN

4 tablespoons	**butter,** divided
2	**boneless, skinless chicken breasts,** cut into bite-size chunks
$\frac{1}{2}$	**small onion,** diced
I tablespoon	**minced garlic**
I tablespoon	**grated fresh gingerroot**
I tablespoon	**curry powder**
I teaspoon	**garam masala**
I teaspoon	**salt**
I cup	**coconut milk**
I tablespoon	**tomato paste**
4–6 cups	**hot cooked rice**

Turn Instant Pot® to Normal Sauté and let heat for I–2 minutes. Melt the butter and place the chicken in a single layer in bottom of pot. Cook for about 3 minutes, or until lightly browned on the bottom. Turn chicken over and cook for I minute; remove to a plate and set aside.

Add the onion to the pot; cook and stir for about 3 minutes, until softened. Add the garlic and ginger and cook, stirring, for I minute. Stir in curry powder, garam masala, and salt; cook for I minute.

In a small bowl, whisk together the coconut milk and tomato paste. Stir coconut milk mixture and reserved chicken into the pot, scraping up browned bits from the bottom. Press Cancel. Place lid on pot and lock into place to seal. Cook on High Pressure for 5 minutes. Use Quick Pressure Release. Stir, and serve over rice.
Makes 4–6 servings.

KUNG PAO CHICKEN

¹/₂ cup	**low sodium soy sauce**
3 tablespoons	**honey**
2 tablespoons	**rice vinegar**
3 cloves	**garlic,** minced
2 tablespoons	**grated fresh gingerroot**
¹/₂ teaspoon	**red pepper flakes**
3 tablespoons	**vegetable oil,** divided
1 ¹/₂ pounds	**boneless, skinless chicken thighs,** cut into 2-inch chunks
¹/₂	**red bell pepper,** diced
1	**small zucchini,** diced
2 tablespoons	**cornstarch mixed with 2 tablespoons water**
4–6 cups	**hot cooked rice,** optional
¹/₂ cup	**roasted salted peanuts**

In a small bowl, stir together the soy sauce, honey, rice vinegar, garlic, ginger, and pepper flakes. Set aside.

Turn Instant Pot® to High Sauté. Add 1 ¹/₂ tablespoons oil and let heat for 1–2 minutes. Add half the chicken to the pot and cook for about 3 minutes, until browned on bottom. Turn chicken pieces and cook for 1 minute; remove to a plate and set aside. Repeat with remaining chicken and 1 ¹/₂ tablespoons oil and then add reserved chicken back to the pot. Stir in soy sauce mixture. Press Cancel.

Place lid on pot and lock into place to seal. Cook on High Pressure for 3 minutes. Use Quick Pressure Release. Press Cancel.

Turn pot to Normal Sauté. Add bell pepper and zucchini; cook for about 2 minutes until vegetables are slightly softened. Stir in cornstarch mixture and cook just until the sauce is thickened. Serve over hot rice, if desired, sprinkled with peanuts. Makes 4–6 servings.

FISH AND
SEAFOOD

VERA CRUZ FISH FILLETS

1 cup	**mild salsa**
1/4 cup	**sliced green olives**
	juice and zest of 1 lime
1/2 cup	**chopped cilantro**
4 (6 ounces each)	**white fish fillets,** such as cod, skin removed
	salt and pepper, to taste

In a small bowl, stir together the salsa, olives, juice, zest, and cilantro. Pour into Instant Pot®. Nestle the fillets into the salsa mixture, leaving the tops bare. Season tops of fillets with salt and pepper.

Place lid on pot and lock into place to seal. Cook on Normal Pressure for 5 minutes. Let sit for 10 minutes. Use Quick Pressure Release. Makes 4 servings.

ASIAN CARAMEL SALMON

2 tablespoons	**vegetable oil**
1/3 cup	**light brown sugar**
I tablespoon	**fish sauce**
I tablespoon	**soy sauce**
I teaspoon	**ginger powder**
	juice and zest of I lime
I pinch	**red pepper flakes**
4 (6 ounces each)	**salmon fillets,** skins removed
	green onions, thinly sliced
	chopped cilantro

Turn Instant Pot® to High Sauté. Place all ingredients except salmon, onions, and cilantro in the pot. Cook for about I minute, stirring, until sugar is dissolved. Press Cancel. Place salmon fillets in the pot on top of the sauce. Place lid on pot and lock into place to seal. Cook on Low Pressure for 8 minutes. Use Quick Pressure Release. Carefully remove fillets with a wide spatula and place on serving plates with bottom sides facing up.

Turn to High Sauté and bring liquid in the pot to a simmer; cook until thickened, about I minute. Brush the salmon with reduced liquid and sprinkle onions and cilantro over top to serve. Makes 4 servings.

MEDITERRANEAN FISH STEW

2 tablespoons	**olive oil**
$\frac{1}{2}$	**medium red onion,** diced
3 cloves	**garlic,** minced
2 tablespoons	**white wine vinegar**
3 cups	**chicken or fish stock**
$\frac{1}{2}$ pound	**fingerling potatoes**
I can (14 ounces)	**diced tomatoes,** with juice
4	**green olives,** sliced
2 tablespoons	**olive brine,** (from jar)
3 (6 ounces each)	**cod fillets,** skins removed
$\frac{1}{2}$	**lemon,** cut in $\frac{1}{4}$-inch-thick slices
$\frac{1}{2}$ cup	**chopped fresh herbs,** such as parsley, basil, or dill

Turn Instant Pot® to High Sauté. Add oil and let heat for about I minute. Add onion and cook for 2–3 minutes, until lightly browned. Add garlic and cook for I minute. Press Cancel. Stir in vinegar, stock, potatoes, tomatoes and juice, olives, and brine. Place cod pieces on top and layer lemon slices over the cod.

Place lid on pot and lock into place to seal. Cook on High Pressure for 10 minutes. Use Quick Pressure Release. Stir, breaking fish into small chunks. Serve garnished with herbs. Makes 4–6 servings.

PECAN CRUSTED HALIBUT

1 tablespoon	**Dijon mustard**
1 tablespoon	**lemon juice**
$^1/_2$ teaspoon	**salt**
4 (6 ounces each)	**halibut fillets**
$^1/_2$ cup	**finely minced or ground pecans**
1 cup	**water**

Mix the mustard, lemon juice, and salt together in a small cup. Brush mixture over 1 side of each fillet. Sprinkle pecans evenly over the mustard mixture on the fillets, pressing to help them adhere to the fish.

Pour water into Instant Pot®. Place wire trivet in pot and arrange the halibut, coated sides up, on top of the trivet. Place lid on pot and lock into place to seal. Cook on Normal Pressure for 12 minutes. Let sit 10 minutes. Use Quick Pressure Release. Makes 4 servings.

TUNA NOODLE CASSEROLE

4 tablespoons	**butter**
½	**large onion,** diced
2 cups	**diced cremini mushrooms**
2 tablespoons	**flour**
I can (12 ounces)	**albacore tuna**
3 cups	**chicken or fish stock**
2 teaspoons	**salt**
I teaspoon	**cayenne pepper sauce**
I cup	**frozen peas**
4 cups (8 ounces)	**uncooked wide egg noodles**
I cup	**sour cream**
I cup	**grated Monterey Jack cheese**
I cup	**crushed potato chips**

Turn Instant Pot® to High Sauté and let heat for about I minute. Add butter and onion. Stir and cook for about 3 minutes, until softened. Add mushrooms and cook for 1–2 minutes until slightly softened. Stir in flour until absorbed and cook for I minute. Drain the liquid from the can of tuna into the pot. Stir in the stock, salt, and hot sauce. Press Cancel. Stir in the peas and noodles.

Place lid on pot and lock into place to seal. Cook on High Pressure for 5 minutes. Let sit for 10 minutes. Use Quick Pressure Release. Taste and add additional salt, if needed. Stir in tuna, sour cream, and cheese until melted. Serve topped with crushed potato chips. Makes 4–6 servings.

SHORTCUT SEAFOOD PAELLA

4 ounces	**Spanish chorizo or andouille sausage,** cut into ¼-inch-thick half-moon slices
1	**small red onion,** diced
1 cup	**uncooked short or medium-grain rice**
1 ½ cups	**chicken or fish stock**
2 teaspoons	**ground turmeric**
1 teaspoon	**cayenne pepper sauce**
1	**red bell pepper,** diced
1 cup	**frozen peas**
12 ounces	**frozen peeled shrimp**
1 (4 ounce)	**frozen white fish fillet,** such as cod
	salt and pepper, to taste

Turn Instant Pot® to Normal Sauté and let heat for 1–2 minutes. Add sausage and onion; stir, and cook for 2–3 minutes, until sausage is lightly browned. Stir in rice. Press Cancel.

Add the stock, turmeric, and pepper sauce; stir, scraping up browned bits from the bottom of the pot. Stir in the bell pepper and peas. Place the shrimp and fish fillet on top of the vegetables; do not stir.

Place lid on pot and lock into place to seal. Cook on High Pressure for 8 minutes. Let sit for 10 minutes. Use Quick Pressure Release. Stir, breaking up the fillet into small chunks and season with salt and pepper. Makes 4–6 servings.

SOUTHERN
SHRIMP AND GRITS

I pound	**medium shrimp,** peeled and deveined
I tablespoon	**Old Bay seasoning**
4 slices	**bacon,** diced
I	**yellow onion,** diced
I	**red bell pepper,** diced
I can (15 ounces)	**crushed tomatoes**
½ cup	**cocktail sauce**
2 tablespoons	**lemon juice**
1½ cups	**water**
1½ cups	**milk**
¾ cup	**stone-ground grits** (not instant or quick)
2 teaspoons	**salt,** plus extra
¼ teaspoon	**pepper,** plus extra
2 tablespoons	**unsalted butter**
¼ cup	**heavy cream**
	green onions, thinly sliced

In a medium bowl, toss the shrimp with the seasoning and set aside.

Turn Instant Pot® to Normal Sauté and let heat for 1–2 minutes. Add the bacon and cook, stirring frequently, until crisp, 4–5 minutes. Remove half of the bacon from the pot and set aside on a paper towel to drain; reserve. Add the onion and pepper and cook, stirring occasionally, until soft and translucent, 3–5 minutes. Stir in the tomatoes, cocktail sauce, and lemon juice, scraping up any browned bits from the bottom of the pot; bring to a simmer. Press Cancel.

In a 6-cup ovenproof glass dish, whisk together the water, milk, grits, 2 teaspoons salt, and ¼ teaspoon pepper. Place wire trivet on top of the sauce mixture in the pot and place dish on top of trivet. Place lid on pot and lock into place to seal. Cook on High Pressure for 12 minutes. Let sit for 10 minutes. Use Quick Pressure Release. Press Cancel.

Remove the dish and the trivet. Whisk the butter and cream into the grits. Stir the shrimp into the sauce in the pot, place lid on pot and allow the residual heat to cook the shrimp through, about 5 minutes, stirring occasionally. Season with salt and pepper, to taste.

To serve, spoon the grits into individual bowls and top with shrimp and sauce. Garnish with reserved bacon and green onions. Makes 4–6 servings.

VEGETARIAN ENTREES

WEEKNIGHT MAC AND CHEESE

16 ounces	**uncooked elbow macaroni**
2 tablespoons	**butter**
4 cups	**water**
1 teaspoon	**salt**
1 can (12 ounces)	**evaporated milk**
8 ounces	**grated sharp cheddar cheese**
1/4 cup	**grated Parmesan cheese**

Add macaroni, butter, water, and salt to Instant Pot®. Place lid on pot and lock into place to seal. Cook on High Pressure for 4 minutes. Use Quick Pressure Release. Stir milk into macaroni and then stir in the cheddar and Parmesan cheese. Place lid back on pot and let sit for 1–2 more minutes. Remove lid and stir until cheeses are melted and combined. Makes 4–6 servings.

VEGAN SOUTHWEST QUINOA BOWLS

1 teaspoon	**extra virgin olive oil**
1/2	**onion,** diced
1	**bell pepper,** seeded and diced
1 teaspoon	**salt**
1 teaspoon	**ground cumin**
1 cup	**uncooked quinoa,** rinsed
1 cup	**salsa,** of choice
1 cup	**water**
1 can (15 ounces)	**black beans,** drained and rinsed
	toppings, of choice, such as, diced avocado, guacamole, fresh cilantro, green onions, salsa, lime wedges, or shredded lettuce, optional

Turn Instant Pot® to Normal Sauté. Add oil and let heat for 1–2 minutes. Add the onion and bell pepper and cook until they start to soften, 2–3 minutes. Stir in salt and cumin and cook for 1 minute. Press Cancel. Add the quinoa, salsa, and water; stir. Place lid on pot and lock into place to seal. Press the Rice button, or cook on Normal Pressure for 10 minutes. Let the pressure release naturally, to make sure the quinoa completely absorbs the liquid.

Fluff the quinoa with a fork and stir in the beans. Serve warm, with desired toppings. Makes 4–6 servings.

CHEESE RAVIOLI LASAGNA

2 cups	**marinara sauce,** of choice
I bag (14 ounces)	**frozen cheese ravioli**
2 cups	**grated Italian blend cheese**
I cup	**ricotta cheese**
1/4 cup	**minced fresh parsley or basil,** or combination
I cup	**water**

Spread 1/2 cup marinara sauce into the bottom of an 8-inch springform pan. Place a single layer of ravioli on top of sauce. Pour 1/2 cup of marinara evenly over ravioli. Sprinkle 1/4 of the Italian blend cheese, 1/4 of the ricotta, and 1/4 of the parsley evenly over top. Repeat 3 more times, for a total of 4 layers of ravioli, ending with sauce and cheese on top. Cover pan loosely with aluminum foil.

Pour water into Instant Pot® and place wire trivet in the bottom of the pot. Set the pan on the trivet. Place lid on pot and lock into place to seal. Cook on Low Pressure for 30 minutes. Let sit for 10 minutes. Use Quick Pressure Release. Let the lasagna rest on the counter for 10 minutes before serving. Makes 4–6 servings.

COCONUT CURRY LENTILS

2 tablespoons	**coconut oil**
1	**medium yellow onion,** finely diced
1	**large stalk celery,** diced
1	**large carrot,** peeled and diced
1 teaspoon	**salt**
1 tablespoon	**curry powder**
2 cups	**green or brown lentils,** rinsed and picked through
2 cloves	**garlic,** minced
1 can (15 ounces)	**diced tomatoes,** with juice
1 can (13.5 ounces)	**coconut milk**
1 cup	**vegetable stock**
	juice of ½ lime
4–6 cups	**hot cooked rice**
	chopped fresh cilantro

Turn Instant Pot® to Normal Sauté. Add the oil and heat for about 1 minute. Add the onion, celery, carrot, and salt; stir and cook until vegetables soften, 3–5 minutes. Add the curry powder, lentils, garlic, tomatoes and juice. Stir in milk and stock. Press Cancel.

Place lid on pot and lock into place to seal. Cook on High Pressure for 5 minutes. Let sit 10 minutes. Use Quick Pressure Release. Stir in the lime juice. Serve over rice and garnish with cilantro. Makes 4–6 servings.

VEGAN MUSHROOM MASALA

½ cup	**roasted, salted cashews**
½	**large onion,** diced
3 cloves	**garlic,** minced
2 tablespoons	**grated fresh gingerroot**
1	**jalapeno pepper,** minced
1 tablespoon	**vegetable oil**
8 ounces	**cremini mushrooms,** cut in ¼-inch-thick slices
1 teaspoon	**salt**
2	**large tomatoes,** diced
½ cup	**vegetable stock**
1 tablespoon	**garam masala**
1 teaspoon	**ground turmeric**
½ cup	**frozen peas**
1 cup	**chopped fresh spinach**
¼ cup	**coconut milk**
4–6 cups	**hot cooked rice**

Soak cashews in 1 cup of boiling water for 15 minutes; drain the water. Place the cashews, onion, garlic, ginger, jalapeno, and a few tablespoons of water in a blender and blend into a puree. Adjust to the consistency of a thick sauce by adding water 1 tablespoon at a time, if necessary.

Turn Instant Pot® to Normal Sauté. Add oil and heat for about 1 minute. Add the puree and cook for 3 minutes, stirring occasionally. Stir mushrooms and salt into pot. Press Cancel. Place lid on pot and lock into place to seal. Cook on High Pressure for 5 minutes. Use Quick Pressure Release.

Place the tomatoes, stock, garam masala, and turmeric in a clean blender and blend until smooth. Add the tomato mixture, peas, spinach, and milk to the pot; stir. Turn pot to High Sauté and bring the mixture to a boil. Press Cancel. Serve over hot rice. Makes 4–6 servings.

PIZZA TOPPED FRITTATA

6	**large eggs,** beaten
I cup	**half-and-half**
I cup	**chopped fresh spinach**
½ cup	**diced tomatoes**
I teaspoon	**salt**
I tablespoon	**minced onion**
½ teaspoon	**garlic powder**
I cup	**water**
I cup	**marinara sauce,** of choice
½ cup	**grated mozzarella cheese**
¼ cup	**grated Parmesan cheese**

In a large bowl, stir together the eggs, half-and-half, spinach, tomatoes, salt, onion, and garlic powder. Pour into a 6-cup round glass dish that has been sprayed with nonstick cooking spray, and cover loosely with aluminum foil.

Pour water into the Instant Pot® and place a wire trivet in the bottom. Set the dish on top of the trivet. Place lid on pot and lock into place to seal. Cook at Normal Pressure for I0 minutes. Let sit for I0 minutes. Use Quick Pressure Release.

Preheat oven broiler.

Invert the frittata onto a baking sheet; if necessary, run a knife around the outside edge of the frittata to loosen. Cover with marinara sauce and sprinkle the cheeses over top. Broil for a few minutes until cheeses melt and start to bubble. Makes 4–6 servings.

LENTIL SLOPPY JOES

I tablespoon	**olive oil**
I	**large onion,** diced
I	**bell pepper,** seeded and diced
I tablespoon	**ground cumin**
I teaspoon	**dried oregano**
3 tablespoons	**ketchup**
I cup	**green or brown lentils,** rinsed and picked through
I cup	**red lentils,** rinsed and picked through
2 cups	**vegetable stock**
I can (15 ounces)	**crushed tomatoes**
2 tablespoons	**Worcestershire sauce**
2 tablespoons	**apple cider vinegar**
6	**hamburger buns,** toasted
6 slices	**cheddar cheese,** optional

Turn Instant Pot® to Normal Sauté. Add the oil and heat for 1–2 minutes. Add the onion and bell pepper and cook for about 2 minutes, until starting to soften. Add cumin, oregano, and ketchup; stir to coat vegetables and cook for another 1–2 minutes. Press Cancel.

Stir in remaining ingredients except for buns and cheese. Place lid on pot and lock into place to seal. Cook on High Pressure for 12 minutes. Let sit for 10 minutes. Use Quick Pressure Release. Serve on hamburger buns with a slice of cheese, if desired. Makes 6 servings.

SHORTCUT STUFFED PEPPERS

4	**medium bell peppers,** any color
I can (14 ounces)	**vegetarian chili**
2	**green onions,** thinly sliced
½ teaspoon	**salt**
I cup	**cooked rice or quinoa**
2 teaspoons	**chili powder**
I tablespoon	**cayenne pepper sauce,** optional
I cup	**grated cheddar cheese,** divided
I cup	**water**

Cut the top ½ inch off of each pepper. Scoop out the seeds and ribs.

In a small bowl, stir together the chili, onions, salt, rice or quinoa, chili powder, and pepper sauce, if using. Mix in ½ of the cheese. Divide and spoon rice mixture into the peppers, leaving I inch at the top.

Place a wire trivet into bottom of Instant Pot® and add the water. Arrange filled peppers on top of the trivet. Place lid on pot and lock into place to seal. Cook on High Pressure for 5 minutes. Let sit 10 minutes. Use Quick Pressure Release. Before removing from pot, sprinkle remaining cheese on top of each stuffed pepper and let melt. Makes 4 servings.

COCONUT CURRY CASHEW RICE

I cup	**uncooked long-grain white rice**
I can (13.5 ounces)	**coconut milk**
I cup	**pineapple juice**
I tablespoon	**Thai red curry paste**
I tablespoon	**cayenne pepper sauce,** optional
I teaspoon	**salt**
I teaspoon	**garlic powder**
I teaspoon	**ground ginger**
	pineapple tidbits
	cashews
	chopped fresh cilantro

Place the rice, milk, juice, curry paste, pepper sauce, if using, salt, garlic powder, and ginger in the Instant Pot®; stir to combine.

Place lid on pot and lock into place to seal. Cook at Normal Pressure for 10 minutes. Let sit for 10 minutes. Use Quick Pressure Release. Serve garnished with pineapple, cashews, or cilantro, as desired. Makes 4–6 servings.

STACKED CHEESE ENCHILADAS

	vegetable oil, for frying
12 (6 inch)	**corn tortillas**
1 cup	**water**
1 can (15 ounces)	**red enchilada sauce**
1 can (8 ounces)	**tomato sauce**
2 teaspoons	**chili powder**
1/2 teaspoon	**salt**
8 ounces	**grated cheddar cheese**
2 ounces	**crumbled queso fresco or feta cheese**
3	**green onions,** thinly sliced

Turn Instant Pot® to Normal Sauté. Add 1 tablespoon oil and let heat for 1–2 minutes. Place 1 tortilla in the pot and cook for about 1 minute on each side, until slightly crisp. Remove tortilla to a paper towel. Repeat with remaining tortillas, adding about 1 teaspoon of oil before cooking each tortilla. Press Cancel. Pour water into the pot.

In a small bowl, whisk together the enchilada sauce, tomato sauce, chili powder, and salt. Pour 1 cup of sauce in the bottom of an 8-inch springform pan. Layer 4 tortillas on top of sauce, overlapping slightly. Pour 1/2 cup of sauce evenly over tortillas. Sprinkle 1/3 of the cheddar, 1/3 of the queso fresco, and 1/3 of the onions over the sauce and tortillas. Repeat this process 2 more times, ending with sauce, cheeses, and onions on top. Cover pan loosely with aluminum foil.

Place the springform pan on a wire trivet and lower into the pot. Place lid on pot and lock into place to seal. Cook on High Pressure for 10 minutes. Use Quick Pressure Release. Let the pan rest on the counter for 10 minutes. Cut into wedges to serve. Makes 4–6 servings.

WARM BEET SALAD

6	**medium red or yellow beets,** (about 3 pounds), scrubbed
I cup	**water**
2 tablespoons	**apple cider vinegar**
2 tablespoons	**extra virgin olive oil**
2 teaspoons	**Dijon mustard**
I teaspoon	**brown sugar**
1/2 teaspoon	**salt**
1/2 cup	**crumbled feta cheese**
1/2 cup	**chopped fresh parsley**
1/2 cup	**chopped walnuts**

Place wire trivet in bottom of Instant Pot® and arrange beets on top. Add water, place lid on pot, and lock into place to seal. Cook on High Pressure for 20 minutes. Let sit for 10 minutes. Use Quick Pressure Release. Remove beets from pot and let sit until cool enough to handle, but still quite warm.

In a small bowl, whisk together the vinegar, oil, mustard, sugar, and salt. When beets are cooled down slightly, peel and cut them into bite-size wedges. Place in a serving dish and drizzle the vinaigrette over top; toss with cheese, parsley, and nuts. Makes 4–6 servings.

SIDE DISHES

LOW MAINTENANCE RISOTTO

4 tablespoons	**butter**
$\frac{1}{2}$	**medium onion,** diced
3 cloves	**garlic,** minced
1$\frac{1}{2}$ cups	**uncooked Arborio rice**
4 cups	**chicken or vegetable stock**
$\frac{1}{4}$ cup	**grated Parmesan cheese**

Turn Instant Pot® to Normal Sauté and let heat for 1–2 minutes. Add butter and onion; stir and cook for about 3 minutes, until onion starts to soften. Add garlic and rice and cook for 1 minute. Add 1 cup of stock and cook, stirring, until stock is absorbed. Press Cancel. Stir in remaining stock and cheese.

Place lid on pot and lock into place to seal. Cook on High Pressure for 10 minutes. Let sit for 10 minutes. Use Quick Pressure Release. Stir before serving. Makes 4–6 servings.

BOSTON STYLE BEANS

16 ounces	**dried small white beans,** such as great Northern
4 ½ cups	**water,** divided
8 slices	**bacon,** diced
½	**large onion,** diced
½	**green bell pepper,** diced
1 can (14 ounces)	**diced tomatoes,** with juice
½ cup	**ketchup**
2 tablespoons	**molasses**
2 tablespoons	**Worcestershire sauce**
1 tablespoon	**yellow mustard**
	salt and pepper, to taste

Pick through beans and remove any small stones or debris. Place beans and 4 cups of water in Instant Pot®. Turn to High Sauté, bring to a boil, and boil for 3 minutes. Empty beans and water into a large bowl and set aside to soak.

Turn pot to Normal Sauté and cook bacon until crispy, 3–4 minutes, stirring frequently. Stir in remaining 1/2 cup water, scraping up any browned bits from bottom of pot. Drain beans and add to the pot along with the remaining ingredients except salt and pepper. Press Cancel.

Place lid on pot and lock into place to seal. Cook on High Pressure for 50 minutes. Let sit 20 minutes. Use Quick Pressure Release. Stir, and season with salt and pepper. Makes 10–12 servings.

FLUFFY MASHED
ROOT VEGETABLES

I pound	**russet potatoes**
I pound	**celery root**
1/2 pound	**sweet potatoes**
4 tablespoons	**butter**
1/2 cup	**water**
1/2 cup	**evaporated milk**
2 teaspoons	**salt**

Peel the potatoes, celery root, and sweet potatoes. Cut all of the vegetables into 2-inch cubes and place in Instant Pot®. Add the butter, water, milk, and salt.

Place lid on pot and lock into place to seal. Cook on High Pressure for I0 minutes. Let sit for I0 minutes. Use Quick Pressure Release. Mash vegetables roughly and then whip with an electric hand mixer at high speed until vegetables are light and fluffy. Makes 6–8 servings.

LEMON-PISTACHIO SPAGHETTI SQUASH

I (2 pound)	**spaghetti squash**
I cup	**water**
1/2 cup	**chopped pistachios**
2 tablespoons	**minced parsley**
3 tablespoons	**butter,** melted
I tablespoon	**lemon zest**
2 tablespoons	**lemon juice**
I teaspoon	**salt**
1/2 teaspoon	**pepper**

Cut squash in half lengthwise; scoop out the seeds and strings. Pour water into Instant Pot® and place a wire trivet in the bottom. Arrange squash halves on top of the trivet, cut sides up. Place lid on pot and lock into place to seal. Cook on High Pressure for 15 minutes. Let sit for 10 minutes. Use Quick Pressure Release. Poke squash halves with a fork to make sure it is tender enough to your liking, but not mushy.

Remove squash to a cutting board. Using a fork, shred the squash from the peel and place in a serving bowl. Add remaining ingredients, stirring gently to combine. Makes 4–6 servings.

BRAISED RED CABBAGE

6 cups (¼-inch-thick)	**red cabbage slices**
½ cup	**water**
1 cup	**applesauce**
¼ cup	**apple cider vinegar**
¼ cup	**brown sugar**
2 teaspoons	**salt**

Add all of the ingredients to the Instant Pot® and stir. Place lid on pot and lock into place to seal. Cook on High Pressure for 12 minutes. Let sit 10 minutes. Use Quick Pressure release. Stir before serving. Makes 4–6 servings.

QUICK POLENTA

1 cup	**polenta or cornmeal** (not instant or quick cooking)
4 cups	**water**
1 teaspoon	**salt**
3 tablespoons	**butter**
½ cup	**finely grated Parmesan cheese**

Turn Instant Pot® to High Sauté. Add polenta, water, and salt; bring to a simmer. Press Cancel. Place lid on pot and lock into place to seal. Cook on High Pressure for 12 minutes. Use Quick Pressure Release.

Whisk in the butter and cheese until melted. Makes 4–6 servings.

SALT CRUSTED FINGERLING POTATOES

4 cups	**hot water**
½ cup	**salt**
2 pounds	**fingerling potatoes, or baby red potatoes**
3 tablespoons	**melted butter,** optional

Add water and salt to Instant Pot®. Whisk until salt is dissolved before adding potatoes. Place lid on pot and lock into place to seal. Cook on High Pressure for 8 minutes. Use Quick Pressure Release. Drain off water.

Spread potatoes on a baking sheet in a single layer and let dry for a few minutes. Serve warm with butter drizzled over top, if desired. Makes 4–6 servings.

CINNAMON ORANGE SWEET POTATOES

2 pounds	**sweet potatoes,** peeled and cut in 1-inch cubes
1 cup	**orange juice**
1 tablespoon	**orange zest**
2 tablespoons	**dark brown sugar**
1/2 teaspoon	**salt**
1/2 teaspoon	**cinnamon**
2 tablespoons	**butter**

Place potatoes in Instant Pot®. Stir in the juice, zest, sugar, salt, and cinnamon. Place lid on pot and lock into place to seal. Cook on High Pressure for 5 minutes. Use Quick Pressure Release. Press Cancel.

Carefully drain any remaining liquid from the pot. Turn pot to High Sauté, and add the butter to the potatoes, gently stirring until melted. Press Cancel. Makes 4–6 servings.

SPEEDY SPANISH RICE

2 tablespoons	**vegetable oil**
1	**medium onion,** diced
½	**bell pepper,** diced
3 cloves	**garlic,** minced
2 cups	**uncooked long-grain white rice**
1 jar (24 ounces)	**mild salsa,** of choice
1 cup	**water**
2 cups	**grated cheddar cheese**
	sliced black olives, optional
	sliced green onions, optional

Turn Instant Pot® to High Sauté, add oil and let heat for about 1 minute. Add onion and bell pepper; stir and cook for 1–2 minutes. Stir in garlic and cook 1 minute. Add rice; stir and cook for 1 minute. Stir in salsa, water, and most of the cheese, reserving a little to garnish. Place lid on pot and lock into place to seal. Cook on High Pressure for 10 minutes. Use Quick Pressure Release.

Spoon rice into a serving bowl and garnish with the reserved cheese, onions, and olives, if desired. Makes 4–6 servings.

TWICE COOKED POTATOES

1 cup	**water**
2 (12 ounces each)	**large russet potatoes**
1/2 cup	**sour cream**
2 tablespoons	**butter,** melted
2 tablespoons	**thinly sliced green onions**
1 cup	**grated sharp cheddar cheese**
1/2 teaspoon	**salt**

Pour water into Instant Pot® and place a wire trivet in the bottom. Pierce potatoes with a fork 2–3 times and arrange on top of trivet. Place lid on pot and lock into place to seal. Cook for 20 minutes on High Pressure. Use Quick Pressure Release. Remove potatoes, cut in half lengthwise, and let sit for a few minutes until cool enough to handle.

Stir together the remaining ingredients in a medium bowl. Scoop the flesh out of the potatoes, leaving a good 1/4-inch-thick shell. Place the potato flesh in a separate bowl and mash with a fork; stir potatoes into the sour cream mixture.

Preheat oven broiler.

Place potato shells on a baking sheet and fill with the potato mixture. Broil until lightly browned and bubbly. Makes 4 servings.

CAULIFLOWER AU GRATIN

1	**large head cauliflower,** core removed
1 cup	**water**
2 tablespoons	**butter**
2 tablespoons	**flour**
1 cup	**milk**
2 teaspoons	**cayenne pepper sauce**
1/2 teaspoon	**salt**
2 cups	**grated sharp cheddar cheese**
1/2 cup	**grated Parmesan cheese,** divided
1/4 cup	**Panko-style breadcrumbs**
1/2 teaspoon	**paprika**

Break up the cauliflower into small florets and place in Instant Pot®. Add water, place lid on pot and lock into place to seal. Cook on Normal Pressure for 1 minute. Use Quick Pressure Release. Press Cancel. Empty cauliflower into a colander and run under cold water to stop cooking, but still leaving cauliflower warm.

Turn pot to Normal Sauté. Add butter and let melt. Whisk in flour and cook for 1 minute. Whisk in milk, pepper sauce, salt, cheddar, and 1/4 cup Parmesan. Cook, whisking constantly, until thickened and cheese has completely melted. Press Cancel. Add cauliflower and stir to coat.

Preheat oven broiler.

Spread cauliflower mixture into an 8 x 10-inch baking dish. Place the remaining 1/4 cup Parmesan, breadcrumbs, and paprika in a food processor; pulse to combine. Sprinkle mixture evenly over the cauliflower. Broil at top of the oven for 2–3 minutes, until crumbs are browned, watching closely so as not to burn. Makes 4–6 servings.

SWEET TREATS

FIVE INGREDIENT FLAN

I cup	**whole milk**
1/2 teaspoon	**cornstarch**
2	**large eggs**
2	**large egg yolks**
I can (14 ounces)	**sweetened condensed milk**
I cup	**water**
1/2 cup	**caramel sauce**

In a small bowl, whisk together the milk and cornstarch until smooth. Add the eggs, egg yolks, and condensed milk; whisk to combine.

Spray a 6–8 cup round glass ovenproof dish with nonstick cooking spray. Pour in the egg mixture and cover dish loosely with aluminum foil. Pour water into Instant Pot®. Place dish on wire trivet and lower into pot. Place lid on pot and lock into place to seal. Cook on Low Pressure for 10 minutes. Let sit for 10 minutes. Use Quick Pressure Release. Place flan in refrigerator and chill for 2 or more hours.

When ready to serve, place caramel sauce in a microwave-safe bowl and heat in microwave until caramel is bubbly around the edges, about 60 seconds. Run a rubber spatula or butter knife around the edges of the flan to loosen. Invert onto a serving platter and drizzle warmed caramel sauce over top. Makes 4–6 servings.

FUDGY CHOCOLATE CAKE

1 cup	**sugar**
1 teaspoon	**vanilla**
1/2 cup	**butter**
2	**large eggs**
3/4 cup	**flour**
1/2 cup	**cocoa powder**
1 teaspoon	**baking powder**
1/2 teaspoon	**salt**
1 cup	**chocolate chips**
1 cup	**water**

In a large bowl with an electric mixer, cream the sugar, vanilla, and butter together until light and fluffy. Beat in eggs, one at a time until well-combined.

In a small bowl, whisk together the flour, cocoa, baking powder, and salt. Slowly add flour mixture to egg mixture until well-combined. Stir in the chocolate chips.

Spray an 8-inch springform pan with nonstick cooking spray. Spoon batter into pan and smooth the top; cover loosely with aluminum foil. Pour water into Instant Pot®. Place wire trivet into the pot and set the pan on top. Place lid on pot and lock into place to seal. Cook on High Pressure for 30 minutes. Let sit 10 minutes. Use Quick Pressure Release. While still warm, cut into wedges and serve.
Makes 4–6 servings.

COCONUT-CINNAMON RICE PUDDING

2 cans (13.5 ounces each) **coconut milk**
1 cup **water**
1 cup **uncooked long-grain white rice**
$\frac{1}{2}$ teaspoon **cinnamon,** or more as desired
$\frac{1}{2}$ cup **sugar**
1 pinch **salt**
$\frac{1}{2}$ cup **raisins,** optional

Add the milk, water, rice, cinnamon, sugar, salt, and raisins, if using, to the Instant Pot® and stir to combine. Place lid on pot and lock into place to seal. Cook on Normal Pressure for 20 minutes. Let sit for 10 minutes. Use Quick Pressure Release. Makes 4–6 servings.

VEGAN LEMON POPPY SEED CAKE

1/2 cup	**coconut oil,** chilled
1/2 cup	**sugar**
1 teaspoon	**vanilla**
2 tablespoons	**lemon juice**
1 tablespoon	**lemon zest**
1 cup	**coconut milk**
2 teaspoons	**baking powder**
1/4 teaspoon	**salt**
2 cups	**flour**
2 tablespoons	**poppy seeds**
1 cup	**water**

In a medium bowl, mix the oil and sugar together with an electric mixer. Add the vanilla, juice, zest, and coconut milk; stir to combine. In a separate bowl, whisk together the baking powder, salt, flour, and poppy seeds. Stir dry mixture into the wet mixture until well-combined.

Spray an 8-inch springform pan with nonstick cooking spray. Spoon batter evenly into pan and cover loosely with aluminum foil. Pour water into Instant Pot® and place wire trivet into the bottom; set pan on top of the trivet. Place lid on pot and lock into place to seal. Cook on High Pressure for 60 minutes. Let sit for 10 minutes. Use Quick Pressure Release. Chill before serving. Makes 6–8 servings.

CLASSIC KEY LIME PIE

I cup	**graham cracker crumbs**
3 tablespoons	**butter,** melted
3	**large egg yolks**
⅔ cup	**lime juice**
I tablespoon	**lime zest,** or more if a stronger lime taste is desired
I can (14 ounces)	**sweetened condensed milk**
¼ cup	**powdered sugar**
I cup	**water**
	sweetened whipped cream

Spray an 8-inch springform pan with nonstick cooking spray. In a small bowl, stir together the cracker crumbs and butter, and then press into the bottom and 2 inches up the sides of the springform pan.

In a medium bowl, whisk together the egg yolks, juice, zest, condensed milk, and sugar. Pour into pan over crust and smooth the top; cover loosely with aluminum foil. Pour water into Instant Pot® and place wire trivet in the bottom; set the pan on top of the trivet.

Place lid on pot and lock into place to seal. Cook on Bake, or High Pressure for 20 minutes. Let the pressure release naturally. Chill in pan for at least 2 hours before serving. Top with whipped cream, to serve. Makes 4–6 servings.

CHOCOLATE CHEESECAKE

1 cup	**chocolate graham cracker crumbs**
3 tablespoons	**butter,** melted
¾ cup	**sugar**
2 packages (8 ounces each)	**cream cheese,** at room temperature
2	**large eggs**
1 tablespoon	**vanilla**
1 tablespoon	**cocoa powder**
1 cup	**chocolate chips,** melted
1 cup	**water**

Spray an 8-inch springform pan with nonstick cooking spray. In a small bowl, stir together the cracker crumbs and butter, and then press into the bottom and 3 inches up the sides of the springform pan.

In a large bowl, beat the sugar and cream cheese together with an electric mixer until light and fluffy. Beat in eggs, one at a time, until well incorporated. Mix in the vanilla, cocoa, and then the melted chocolate chips until well-combined. Pour into pan over crust and smooth the top; cover loosely with aluminum foil. Pour water into Instant Pot® and place wire trivet in the bottom; set the pan on top of the trivet.

Place lid on pot and lock into place to seal. Cook on High Pressure for 45 minutes. Let sit for 10 minutes. Use Quick Pressure Release. Chill in pan 4–24 hours before serving. Makes 4–6 servings.

RAVE REVIEWS CHEESECAKE

⅓ cup	**chopped pecans**
⅔ cup	**graham cracker crumbs**
½ teaspoon	**cinnamon**
3 tablespoons	**butter,** melted
2 packages (8 ounces each)	**cream cheese,** at room temperature
⅔ cup	**sugar**
¼ cup	**sour cream**
2	**large eggs**
I teaspoon	**cornstarch**
I teaspoon	**vanilla**
I cup	**water**

Spray an 8-inch springform pan with nonstick cooking spray. Pulse the pecans in a food processor or blender until very fine crumbs. In a small bowl, stir together the pecans, cracker crumbs, cinnamon, and butter. Press into bottom and 2 inches up the sides of the springform pan.

In a separate bowl, beat the cream cheese and sugar together with an electric mixer until very smooth. Beat in the sour cream, eggs, cornstarch, and vanilla until well-combined and smooth. Pour into pan over crust and smooth the top; cover loosely with aluminum foil.

Pour water into Instant Pot® and place wire trivet in the bottom; set the pan on top of the trivet. Place lid on pot and lock into place to seal. Cook on High Pressure for 30 minutes. Let pressure release naturally for at least 20 minutes. Chill in pan at least 2 hours before serving. Makes 4–6 servings.

UPSIDE DOWN BERRY COBBLER

1 cup	**flour**
6 tablespoons	**butter,** divided
½ cup	**sugar,** divided
2 teaspoons	**baking powder**
¼ teaspoon	**salt**
¼ teaspoon	**baking soda**
½ cup	**buttermilk**
4 cups	**mixed fresh berries,** such as blueberries, raspberries, and blackberries
3 tablespoons	**cornstarch**
1 cup	**orange juice**
	vanilla ice cream, optional

Place the flour and 4 tablespoons butter in a food processor and pulse into small crumbs. Add ¼ cup sugar, baking powder, salt, and baking soda; pulse a few times to combine. Drizzle in buttermilk and continue to pulse until mixture just comes together. Spread the remaining 2 tablespoons butter evenly into the bottom of the Instant Pot®. Spoon batter into pot, spreading evenly to completely cover the bottom.

In a medium saucepan, combine berries, cornstarch, juice, and remaining ¼ cup sugar. Bring to a simmer and let cook for 1 minute, smashing about half of the berries while mixture is simmering. Pour hot berry mixture evenly over the top of the batter.

Place lid on pot and lock into place to seal. Cook on High Pressure for 20 minutes. Let sit for 10 minutes. Use Quick Pressure Release. Spoon into bowls with the berry mixture on the bottom and the browned batter on top. Serve immediately topped with a scoop of vanilla ice cream, if desired. Makes 4–6 servings.

WALNUT BANANA CAKE

½ cup	**butter,** at room temperature
½ cup	**sugar**
½ cup	**light brown sugar**
1 teaspoon	**vanilla**
2	**very ripe bananas**
¼ cup	**plain yogurt**
1	**large egg**
1 ¼ cups	**flour**
¼ teaspoon	**salt**
1 teaspoon	**cinnamon**
1 teaspoon	**baking soda**
1 teaspoon	**baking powder**
½ cup	**chopped walnuts, mixed with 2 tablespoons brown sugar**
1 cup	**water**

Place the butter, sugar, light brown sugar, and vanilla in a bowl, and beat with a mixer on high speed until fluffy, about 3 minutes. In a small bowl, mash 1 of the bananas and part of the other, if necessary, to make 1 cup. Add mashed banana, yogurt, and egg to butter mixture; beat on low to incorporate.

In a small bowl, whisk together the flour, salt, cinnamon, baking soda, and baking powder. Cut the remaining banana into ¼-inch-thick half-moon slices. Add to the flour mixture and gently stir to coat. Stir the flour mixture into the wet mixture until combined. Spray an 8-inch springform pan with nonstick cooking spray. Pour batter into pan. Sprinkle walnut mixture over top, pressing lightly into batter. Cover pan loosely with aluminum foil. Pour water into Instant Pot® and place wire trivet into the bottom; set pan on top of the trivet. Place lid on pot and lock into place to seal. Cook on Cake setting or Normal Pressure for 60 minutes. Let sit for 10 minutes. Use Quick Pressure Release. Let cake cool to warm before serving. Makes 4–6 servings.

MIRACLE STRAWBERRY JAM

2 pounds	**ripe strawberries**
	juice and zest of ½ lemon
I cup	**sugar**

Wash, gently dry, and hull strawberries. Place stawberries in bowl of food processor and pulse until small bits. Add strawberries to Instant Pot® and stir in the juice and zest, and sugar; let sit for 30 minutes.

Place lid on pot and lock into place to seal. Cook at Medium Pressure for 5 minutes. Let the pressure release naturally all the way. Place jam in a covered container and chill at least 2 hours before serving to allow jam to thicken. Makes 2 cups.

EFFORTLESS DULCE DE LECHE

I can (14 ounces) **sweetened condensed milk**

Peel label off the can and place unopened can on its side in the Instant Pot®. Fill the pot with water up to I inch above the can.

Place lid on pot and lock into place to seal. Cook on High Pressure for 40 minutes. Let sit for 10 minutes. Use Quick Pressure Release. Remove the can with tongs and let sit on countertop until cooled to warm. Open and serve over ice cream, as a fruit or cookie dip, or drizzled over waffles. Makes 1 ¼ cups.

PINEAPPLE UPSIDE DOWN CAKES

1 cup	**pineapple juice**
1/4 cup	**vegetable oil**
3	**large eggs**
1 box (15 ounces)	**yellow or butter cake mix**
1/4 cup	**butter,** melted
1/2 cup	**brown sugar**
6	**canned pineapple rings**
6	**maraschino cherries**
1 cup	**water**

In a medium bowl, mix together the juice, oil, and eggs using an electric mixer. Add the cake mix and continue mixing on low speed until combined.

Divide the melted butter into each of 6 (8-ounce) ramekins; swirling to coat the bottoms. Sprinkle a little brown sugar evenly over the butter, covering completely. Place 1 pineapple ring on top of brown sugar and drop a cherry into the center of each ring. Pour 1/2 cup of batter into each ramekin, smooth the tops, and cover loosely with aluminum foil.

Pour water into Instant Pot® and place wire trivet into the bottom. Arrange 3 of the ramekins on top of the trivet. Arrange the remaining ramekins in the pot, alternating the placement so they straddle the ramekins on the bottom. Place lid on pot and lock into place to seal. Cook on High Pressure for 8 minutes. Let sit 10 minutes. Use Quick Pressure Release.

Let ramekins sit for a few minutes on the counter to cool to warm. Run a knife around outside edges of each cake and invert onto individual serving plates. Makes 6 servings.

CINNAMON ROLL
BREAD PUDDING

I package (24 ounces)	**unfrosted cinnamon rolls*** (about 8 rolls)
3	**large eggs**
¼ cup	**sugar**
¼ cup	**butter,** melted
I teaspoon	**vanilla**
I cup	**milk**
½ cup	**raisins,** optional
½ cup	**chopped nuts,** of choice, optional
I cup	**water**

Cut cinnamon rolls into 2-inch cubes; you should have 8 cups of cubes. Spread on a baking sheet and let dry overnight. In a large bowl, whisk together eggs, sugar, butter, vanilla, and milk. Toss dried cubes into egg mixture and let sit a few minutes; toss again. Repeat this process until most of the liquid has been absorbed. Toss in raisins and nuts, if using.

Spray an 8-inch springform pan with nonstick cooking spray. Spoon bread mixture into the pan and cover loosely with aluminum foil. Pour water into Instant Pot® and place wire trivet in the bottom. Set the pan on top of the trivet. Place lid on pot and lock into place to seal. Cook on High Pressure for 20 minutes. Let sit 10 minutes. Use Quick Pressure Release. Makes 4–6 servings.

*Note: I buy my unfrosted cinnamon rolls at the local grocery store in their bakery department. If that option is not available to you, scrape off excess frosting before cutting into cubes and drying. To speed up the drying process, preheat oven to 200 degrees and bake cinnamon roll cubes for 20 minutes, stirring halfway through baking time.

CINNAMON RED HOTS®
APPLESAUCE

2 pounds	**apples,** sweet and tart variety mixed
½ cup	**water**
½ cup	**sugar**
2 tablespoons	**cinnamon Red Hots® candy**

Peel, core, and cut apples into 1-inch chunks; place in Instant Pot®. Add the water, sugar, and candy; stir.

Place lid on pot and lock into place to seal. Cook on High Pressure for 5 minutes. Let sit for 10 minutes. Use Quick Pressure Release. Use a potato masher to mash cooked apples into an applesauce texture. Chill for at least 2 hours before serving. Makes 4–6 servings.

EVERYBODY'S FAVORITE CARAMEL CORN

2 tablespoons	**coconut oil**
2 tablespoons	**butter**
½ cup	**popcorn kernels**

Caramel Sauce

4 tablespoons	**butter**
½ cup	**light brown sugar**
½ teaspoon	**salt**
2 tablespoons	**light corn syrup**
¼ teaspoon	**baking soda**

Turn Instant Pot® to High Sauté. Add oil and butter and heat for about 1 minute until they begin to shimmer. Add kernels. While pot is still turned to High Sauté, place lid on pot but do not seal. Let cook for about 2 minutes, until display on pot reads "Hot." Press Cancel. You will hear kernels continuing to pop. Wait 1–2 minutes until you no longer hear popping. Open lid and empty the popped corn into a large paper bag.

For the Caramel Sauce, turn Instant Pot® to High Sauté. Add butter and let melt. Stir in the sugar, salt, and corn syrup and bring to a boil; boil for 1 minute. (Note: 1 minute of cooking time will yield a soft, gooey texture. If you like your caramel corn crunchy, let this mixture boil for 4 minutes.) Press Cancel.

Remove the inner pot and whisk in the baking soda. Pour the caramel sauce immediately into the paper bag over the popcorn, seal the bag at the top by folding over, and shake vigorously. Spread caramel corn on an oiled baking sheet and let cool before serving. Makes about 8 cups.

NOTES

METRIC CONVERSION CHART

Volume Measurements

U.S.	Metric
1 teaspoon	5 ml
1 tablespoon	15 ml
1/4 cup	60 ml
1/3 cup	75 ml
1/2 cup	125 ml
2/3 cup	150 ml
3/4 cup	175 ml
1 cup	250 ml

Weight Measurements

U.S.	Metric
1/2 ounce	15 g
1 ounce	30 g
3 ounces	90 g
4 ounces	115 g
8 ounces	225 g
12 ounces	350 g
1 pound	450 g
2 1/4 pounds	1 kg

Temperature Conversion

Fahrenheit	Celsius
250	120
300	150
325	160
350	180
375	190
400	200
425	220
450	230

 Check out these "101" favorites
for more tasty recipes:

Bacon	**More Bacon**
BBQ	**More Ramen**
Beans	**More Slow Cooker**
Beer	**Pumpkin**
Cake Mix	**Ramen Noodles**
Canned Biscuits	**Rice**
Casserole	**Sheet Pan**
Chile Peppers	**Slow Cooker**
Chocolate	**Toaster Oven**
Dutch Oven	**Tortilla**
Grits	**Tots**

Each 128 pages, $9.99

Available at bookstores or directly from GIBBS SMITH
1.800.835.4993
www.gibbs-smith.com

ABOUT THE AUTHOR

Donna Kelly is a dedicated foodie, passionate home cook, recipe developer and cookbook author. She competed serval years at the annual World Food Championships. She is a regular guest cook on Utah morning television show cooking segments and has appeared on Martha Stewart's Sirius radio show, *Everyday Food*. She is the author of several cookbooks including *French Toast*, *Burritos*, and *Quesadillas*. Donna has been an attorney for more than 32 years, primarily as a prosecutor handling sex crimes, domestic violence, and child abuse cases. She is a mom to five adult children and lives in Utah with her husband of 40 years.